# PLANETARY
# INITIATION

## Rita Milios

Tools for Transformation Press
Toledo, Ohio

# Planetary Initiation
Copyright © 1995  Rita Milios

**Publisher's Cataloging in Publication** (Prepared by Quality Books Inc.)

Milios, Rita.  4/98
    Planetary initiation / Rita Milios.
    p. cm.
    ISBN 0-9641657-0-8

    1. Spiritual life.  I. Title.

BL624.M55 1994                                                291.4
                              QBI94-1218


Cover, design and electronic publishing:
Chris Willis / Media 1
11738 Apple Drive • Nunica, MI 49448-9762
616.837.6119


First Edition, First Printing March, 1995
Printed in the United States of America

**Tools for Transformation Press**
7150 Cloister Rd. W. • Toledo, OH 43617
419.841.4657

*To Light Group 359,*

*With special thanks to*

*Denise & Jenny*

# Contents

# Introduction

Dear Reader:

Something is happening. You can feel it in the air. Something new is taking place around you and *to* you. Perhaps you have noticed "something strange" going on, something that started several years ago and seems to be picking up speed at an amazing pace. That something involves change - change in every sense of the word.

Perhaps people you know have been acting differently. They may seem more anxious, in a hurry to "move on with their lives," but they aren't quite sure what that means. You may feel the same way, too. You may notice some strange things happening to your body as well. Sometimes your nerves may feel "jangled," and you feel like you just drank ten cups of coffee. You may feel depressed or unusually tired - bone weary. You may find that you are more forgetful and that you have trouble keeping a mental focus.

These strange bodily sensations are just a few of the symptoms caused by what I have come to call "the New Energy" coming into our midst. This new energy is coming to Earth for the first time ever, traveling from a far off universe that most people probably don't even know exists.

These are exciting times. This moment in history has been awaited by the prophets and seers for thousands of years. We are experiencing a turning of the spiral of evolution - one that has *never before* been possible.

I began to learn of the specialness of this current time period in 1990 when I and another of my fellow Light Group members began channeling information about the upcoming changes. At first I was reluctant to "buy into" the messages we were getting. But subsequent communications with another highly evolved Light Group in Texas confirmed our messages. In fact, they were almost identical!

As the events that were told to us began to unfold in amazing accuracy, I began to realize just how important they were, and how important it was that I fulfill my role in the "drama" that was unfolding. For not only had I (and others) been given messages, we were given jobs to do as well. This book is part of my commitment to do that job, and to do my part to bring about the working out of the Plan on Earth.

I have been a spiritual teacher for eight years, carefully, almost reluctantly, teaching deeper and deeper esoteric truths, as year by year it seemed that more and more revelation was needed. I only recently made a jump in my own spiritual evolution, taking what is called an *Initiation* of a certain number or degree, and since then have been moved, not always willingly, into even greater service. The responsibilities of the spiritual Path grow heavy as one climbs higher, yet the joys always outweigh the responsibilities, and the truth is that I would never think even for a moment of *not* continuing on my Path. Still, I wonder at times, "Will I be able to do it all? Am I really being guided?" Always I come to know, eventually, that the answers are "Yes."

Today, with this book, I introduce the first of what I hope to become many books on the esoteric truths that I have learned and taught others. These books will present information that is *needed* right now by the average man or woman on the street, by the seeker, by those just entering the Path and by those who have traveled a ways on the Path and are now finding that they, too, are facing an advanced Initiation.

I have always felt that my place is at the midway point, between the Masters and the average person, new to the Path. With one foot in each universe, I share my experience and understanding, in the hopes that it will make the way easier for the ones following, and in the hopes that they, too, will feel the commitment to discover and take up their own "jobs."

I am "coming out into the open" with these books that contain many ideas and messages that I have heretofore expressed only to my fellow Group members and have just very recently begun sharing with my students. I have not been concerned that others might not understand or agree with what I say; instead I have always felt that certain lessons cannot be taught. After a certain point, one has to *experience* them, so teaching about them is difficult. This is still true, but I feel now that because things are moving so quickly that there needs to be a better understanding of the rather unsettling changes that are happening to numbers of people. I know from experience, for example, that the registering of the new energies in one's body can bring about great havoc, to the point where some people believe that they are losing their minds or "coming unglued." People need to know what is happening to them and how to best handle it.

In addition, I have come to see that some of my own "rules" for how I taught and shared my spiritual growth experiences (such as channeling) were perhaps too rigid. For instance, I had a "rule," only recently broken, that no one, other than those involved, knew that I channeled at all. Furthermore, I would only channel for my own group, and for the purposes of learning the next "task" that we were to be given. Part of the reason for this was that I have always felt that communication with one's Masters was somehow "sacred" and that this ability to communicate must never be "cheapened" or "degraded" by making it a "sideshow" event.

Over the last year, though, I have been led to understand that these were *my* limitations, placed on me *by me,* and that while honorable useful and for a time, they have now, because of new circumstances, come to the point where they are actually holding me back from fulfilling my mission and further treading my Path.

I have always been led intuitively, from an early age, to know what it is that I must do next, from the early commands of "get yourself together" to more recently suddenly and unexpectedly being led to embark on yet another new career (as a social worker) and now to finally and fully "come out into the open" with my spiritual beliefs and teachings. In following my Path, I find that one thing naturally leads into the other. I see now why I spent so many years studying psychology and science, why I became a writer and learned about the publishing world (even if it was mainly through children's books and textbooks), why I came to teach and to become a professional speaker. All these learnings are now brought together in my current work. They allow me to give my *newest* gifts, to continue as I was meant to do, learning first, then sharing with others what I learned; first helping myself, then helping others.

Several years ago, when the "change" first stated to take place within my mind and body - when I first began my movement to the new spiritual level - I had in my meditations a reoccurring visualization. I was climbing a steep hill, along with the other members of my group (which at time included at least seven people, and at times as many as twelve). As we climbed higher, people began to drop back. Soon, as I approached a great wall, there were but three of us left. With difficulty, I managed to scale the wall, and looking back, I saw the remaining two trying to scale it also. I reached down and gave them my hand. When we three were over, I looked back again, sadly, knowing that the others would not - at least at this time - be joining us.

Our Light Group in the end dwindled to the three of us and with the force of our commitment to the Plan we grew together, gaining new master guides and channeling in a totally new way. In the final stages (for this group, too, eventually disbanded) we learned that our time together was indeed coming to a close as it was time that we went out into the world and shared our various gifts. As it was said to me many times in meditation and through channeled messages, we were to "Go out into the world and BE." I now know what this "BEing" means.

As I became more involved with helping people one on one, and as I encountered more people through my work, I began to sense that something was different about the way they responded to me. At first, I was perplexed, because although I had always been well liked and had a lot of friends, suddenly I felt as people were being *drawn* to me. People seemed to be sensing my expanding Light and responding to it. I came to expect this reaction and soon was no longer surprised by it.

It did bring with it, though, a sense of still greater responsibility, as I received messages that I (and others like me) were, by our very physical presence, acting as "step-down" units for the new energy. One of our jobs was to take in the new energy (which we were better able to handle, having already made the "changeover") and step down its frequency for those around us. This would occur as our auras intermingled during ordinary daily activities. So the injunction to "Go out into the world and BE."

Another reason for the injunction was so that we could be living examples for the new pattern, the new frequency, the *new way of being* that was being created by the new energy. And that is what this book is all about.

In this book I have tried to give you a "preview" of what is immediately ahead for many of you. It is an exciting but sometimes difficult journey, full of "tests" and necessitating a complete "letting go" of of that which has for so long been most familiar and dear - your beliefs about who you really are. You will be moving from a viewpoint of seeing yourself as a person(ality) to seeing yourself as a soul, with all its multiply-incarnated "parts" (some of which whose origins may surprise you greatly). You will be moving from acting and *being* a person(ality) to *being a soul*.

This is your mission. I hope that you find some guidance and solace in these pages and that my "signposts" can help you as you tread the Path.

Perhaps I'll see you at the next waystation.....

# CHAPTER 1

# WHAT'S GOING ON HERE?

These are exciting and tumultuous times. Many changes are taking place in the world. Because of certain universal and earthly alignments, the current time period is "ripe" for mankind to make a new turn on the evolutionary and spiritual spiral, for our soul natures to begin to "wake up" and to take charge of this new leap in evolution.

This turning of the spiral is related to time and space "cycles" which align approximately every 2,000 years. It is also related to an even greater universal cycle which is in turn related to certain "superuniverse" cycles which have to do with events and Purposes that we as humans can never even conceive. Messages from our spiritual Masters and the sacred writings about the "ageless wisdom" in esoteric books like the *Vedas* and more recently the writings of Master Djwhal Khul in *The Alice Bailey Books* give us clues to the unfolding drama that lies just ahead.

There is, indeed, "something strange" going on today. As

this evolutionary new spiral readies itself for "the turn," there is a new arrival on our planet of *new* energy from space - an energy that has come from beyond our known universe. Scientists in the past two years have recognized this energy and called it "cosmic rays" of an unknown origin. They have determined that it is coming from beyond our known universe, from where or what was previously thought to be "empty" space. This new energy is causing some consternation among scientists as they try to figure out what it is and what it is doing here. But, even more than that, it is causing consternation among us, the people of the earth who are experiencing its effects on our bodies.

## THE EFFECTS OF THE NEW ENERGY

I have personally experienced strange happenings within my own body and mind, which were later revealed to have been effects of the new energy. Since that time (almost 2 years ago), I have heard of many other people who are experiencing "strange symptoms" and don't know what is happening to them. Many of these people are not what I would normally call "New Agers," but people who are, nonetheless, connected to their spiritual natures in a definite and conscious way. In their own manner, they are treading the Path. (And that is perhaps worth remembering. Not all spiritual growth goes on under the direction of "New Age" methods.) Also affected are the "true" New Age or New Thought participants who are consciously attached to the philosophies of the esoteric teachings. These people, who do tend to be in the "fast lane" spiritually speaking, are often affected in a more direct and profound way, as they may be taking an "advanced" Initiation or moving to a higher turn on the spiral than the "average" person, at least at this time.

From the experiences of myself, my fellow meditation group members, a "sister" group in Texas, and a number of hypnotherapy clients and friends, I have put together the following list of "symptoms" that appear to herald the presence of the new energy within one's body.

This list is in no way complete, as symptoms seem to vary from one individual to another (perhaps due to differences in physical or emotional health, and differences in the blockages of chakra energy). Persons would not expect to have all of these symptoms (at least, let's hope not!) and some may be more profound in one person than in another. This list is not given to in any way "diagnose" a problem, and you are urged not to use it to either diagnose yourself or someone else. Many of these symptoms are also symptoms of physical illnesses, so please see your doctor if you have any of the physical symptoms. But do be aware that these same symptoms have been "reported" by people who are responding to the new energy by also experiencing acceleration in their spiritual growth. If you have experienced any of these following symptoms, you *may* be reacting to the new energy. This does not mean that you won't require medical treatment, it simply means that *in addition*, you may want to be aware of what you can do *spiritually* to lessen the degree of the effects of the new energy and to move through the "change" as quickly as possible.

- *A "jazzed" feeling* (The best way that I can describe this is that you feel as though you have just had your finger plugged into an electric socket, or you have just drunk ten cups of double strength caffeinated coffee. Your whole body feels "electrified" or "charged.")

- *Feelings of your skin "crawling" or itching for no known reason* (This also relates to the *jazzed* feeling above.)

- *Ringing in the ears* (This is the "sound" of the higher frequency.)

- *Forgetfulness* (A very common comment - this is the kind of forgetfulness involved with "tip of the tongue" syndrome, where you know something but can't retrieve it from memory.)

- *Communication problems* (Not being able to make others understand you is the most common complaint. Also reported is not being able to understand other points of view. Many relationship "fallouts" have occurred over this one.)

- *Heart palpitations* (Be *sure* to see your doctor!) This symptom is very serious and should be monitored by a doctor, even if there seems to be no physical reason for it.

- *Unexplained nosebleeds* (May be a sign of an alien implant. See Chapter 7.)

- *Tingling or throbbing in the palms of hands or in feet* (The energy is entering here.)

- *Fogginess* (A feeling of mental fog; also a lack of mental focus.)

- *Excessive dreaming* ("Lessons" are being delivered; many people awaken with a vague feeling of having been "taught" all night long.)

- *Sudden onset of fearfulness; near paranoia* (Fears that were once hidden are now being brought to the surface.)

- *A resurgence of old emotional problems* (Similar to above; all negativity must now be removed from our minds and hearts.)

- *Being drawn to nature* (Suddenly appreciating nature; feeling a connection.)

- *Seeing auras* (For those who have not normally seen them; or an increase in the ability to see them for those who do.)

- *A new or expanded sense of purpose* (More and more people moving onto the Path.)

These are the symptoms that I have run across. There may be more. Remember, you do not have to experience all or even most to be experiencing the effects of the new energy. Each person's experience will be unique, as each one's life is at a different stage, each has experienced different learnings, and each has different emotional "baggage" left to work through. Some people experience more physical symptoms while others experience more psychological ones. Some experience a combination of both.

There do seem to be some similarities, though, especially when one is nearing the "end" and begins to be readied for the next level of spiritual commitment. When you have successfully weathered the changes, have proven to be "teachable" and have therefore received some initial "programming" (which comes, as I said, through dreams, and also through meditation and intuition) then you will be ready to receive what I call the "Initiation Ceremony."

I have participated in my own Initiation Ceremony, that of my fellow group members and interestingly enough, through hypnotherapy, have helped to facilitate several other initiations. These last ones came at first as somewhat of a surprise, but later as I realized what was happening, this avenue for spiritual growth made a lot of sense. Many people come to me for hypnotherapy to work out issues or conflicts in their lives. They typically feel that there is something that is "holding them back." Because of my own spiritual nature and the other work that I do (teaching spiritual classes, writing spiritual books, etc.) I am in contact with many other people who also are of a spiritual nature. It is only natural that when such people come for hypnotherapy that this spiritual aspect will come out in the therapy.

Our subconscious minds hold not only our conflicts and problems, they hold also our inner resources, and are, in fact, our spiritual connection, bridging our individual consciousnesses with the Universal Consciousness. As I work with people I use whatever belief system that they hold to help them to reach these inner resources and make them available in their everyday lives. If a person believes in guides, angels or Masters, these positive resources are used to help the person resolve their conflicts and to empower themselves. (This may or may not include a past life experience.)

What I have found is that when highly spiritual people come to me for help, they are often in the throes of the "changeover," or transformation process, and because of this are experiencing inner conflict as they shed the last vestiges of their negativity - doubts, fears, old conflicts, past relationships and any elements of their "dark side" that have yet to be cleansed. This must all take place before they can move to the next level of spiritual growth and receive their Initiation. This is not to say that it must be *finished*, for in truth, we probably are never finished, at least not as long as we have human incarnations. But the work must have *begun* and it must have been *committed* to. As long as the person is working on the tasks of the next level, he or she is "initiated" to that level, the idea being, I assume, that we are trusted to continue the work as we have "proven" ourselves capable and committed.

As the spiritual person resolves her conflicts, she is, in effect, removing the last obstacles to her next steps on the Path. When this happens, especially if we have been working with guides or spiritual images in the hypnotherapy, it is only natural that these guides will take the opportunity to perform the "welcoming ceremony." But not only is it a welcome to the next level, it is a time of promising and committing to the tasks associated with the next level. It is both an exciting event and a sobering event, as the person realizes the increased responsibilities that are expected of her. But, as is always the case, the joys outweigh any "heaviness" felt by the new responsibilities.

After several had people have reached this point and were reporting in their hypnotic images visions associated with initiation, I began to be aware of the signs that people showed when they were experiencing this event as part of their therapy. Because the initiation "ritual" seems to contain a number of similarities no matter who is experiencing it, I have begun to believe that there are "standard" images that are indicative of the true initiation process.

One of the first clues that this is about to happen is that clients report symptoms of receiving the new energy - especially the tingling in the extremities and the "fogginess" or loss of focus. Other symptoms might be present as well. It was often difficult at first to separate these symptoms from the client's other presenting problems, but eventually they would say or report something that indicated that a spiritual transformation was about to take place in their lives. (Having dreams of people talking to them and teaching them, for example.) I usually wait until there are signs that the initiation process itself is underway to discuss the signs in detail with clients so as not to "pre-program" them through hypnosis. By this time, their angels and Masters will have already given the client much of the information through visualizations and I need simply to elaborate on it and clarify it for them. There is always a *decision* that must be made, and this decision (to commit to the Path) must be made by the person with their full understanding and *conscious agreement.* Once they have decided to commit to their Path, I feel free to help them to understand more about what lies ahead.

The Initiation Ceremony often consists of several *very tall* Archangels being present around the person (usually in a circle). The term "tall" has become a clear clue. These Angels usually express joy in some manner, a kind of celebration for the person having "arrived" in their midst. This might be in the form of a jubilant "dance" or other movement, or it might simply be in the form of an intense feeling of being surrounded by love and joy and peace. Then one or several of the Angels often speaks to the person and tells them of their accomplishment, and how they might now expect to be freed of all that in the past has held them back. They are told that they are now on their Path. They are sometimes shown what they might expect on that Path. Some clients have been shown signs of new "jobs" that they will be doing. Others simply visualized being on a golden Path where all was sparking and light and peacefulness. These were told that they would get the information that they needed as they needed it, through their intuition, so they should listen for it. Most were asked directly if they accepted this Path, if they willingly and consciously committed to it. If they answered "yes" (and I have not had anyone who refused) then they were again congratulated, blessed and told the next step that they needed to take to immediately begin to follow that Path. The process varies, but these are the basic elements.

For many people, the ceremony is not the end of their "cleansing." They still have to finish clearing out the emotional blocks, releasing all past karma and negativity. But the ceremony seems to be a turning point. Some clients who had believed that their fears were almost too great to be overcome were now able to trust that they could and would overcome them. They had seen their immediate spiritual "future" and because of its positiveness were able to allow themselves to walk into it. It then seemed that once their spiritual selves were "elevated" that the other "selves" - emotional, physical and mental - were able to quickly follow.

As I said, these were the experiences of people who had their initiation ritual within the framework of a hypnotherapy session. But others, of course, will receive their initiation in other frameworks, often during a meditation session. Their experiences may vary from those above, but probably some similarities will exist. Let me now share with you the Initiation Ceremony that myself and two other Light Group members experienced almost two years ago. This ceremony was also reported by our "sister" group in Texas. But by the time we received their news, much of our ceremony had already taken place. (It happened over a time period of several weeks and included several rituals.) This similarity between our respective experiences served to validate each of them, because we knew that we had not simply "copied" one another but had instead actually received nearly identical initiations.

After having been "told" (through meditation and channeling) for a number of months that "something big" was about to happen, we began to experience changes within our group. The first sign was a loss of time during meditation. We usually meditated for about ten to twenty minutes and I for one was never completely "out of touch" during these periods. At some level I was always aware that I was still in my house (or another home) and that I was in meditation. I could arouse myself at will as needed (for instance if the phone suddenly interrupted the meditation, which can really be a shock to one's system!). Yet, suddenly in our meditations we would all at the same time be "out" for forty to forty minutes, returning to our waking awareness totally shocked that we had been out of touch with "reality" for that long (it felt like about ten minutes) and also unable to remember anything that happened while we were "gone." This didn't go over very well with me at first, because I like to always know what is going on and what is being done to me. But we were reassured that we were being "prepared" and that all would be well. The "blackouts" were evidentially necessary to re-program us to receive the higher vibrations of the new energies, as our bodies could not in normal awareness stand these higher frequencies.

At the same time, the two of us who channeled received information that we would be doing that in a different way, and indeed, we did begin to manifest changes in the way the entities "connected" with us. Previously I had always felt a "wafting down" of the energy of the "speaker," sort of "overlaying" my body, especially the head and throat area. After the "re-programming" I felt that instead of the energies being reduced down to my frequency, my energies were being elevated, raising my frequency to theirs (or at least closer to it - perhaps we met one another halfway in between). This evaluation was later validated in our messages.

Subsequently, we also began to receive "flames" as symbols of new commitments and responsibilities. We were led to join in a circle and in meditation each of us "received" a flame of a particular color. These flames were perceived as colors of energy, being handed to us by an Archangel and deposited into our heart chakras. I cannot recall the exact order, but one by one the flames were presented over a period of several weeks. The blue flame, presented by Gabriel, was the flame of healing and compassion. The magenta flame was the flame of vitality and life, and was presented by Raphael. The pink flame was the flame of unconditional love, the indigo the flame of synthesis, the yellow for releasing the karma of past lives. The orange flame was soothing, a calming to our "excited" energy systems, and the gold flame was our call to action, representing our participation in the wisdom, truth and beauty of the spiritual Path. Other angels - Azriel, Uriel and more - took part in the ongoing ritual and each welcomed us into their realm and thanked us for our willingness to participate in the unfolding of the Plan and the Purpose of Earth.

As we received the flames, several of our chakras were blended - the throat chakra blending with the heart chakra and the third eye, the first two chakras moving up to join the third, and finally all the chakras joining into one large "stargate" within the heart. This represented our expanded capacities to "wield our energies" and resulted in our "shining forth" greatly (I am convinced that it is this Light that others - on a soul level - see that makes them drawn to me.) One of the respon-

sibilities of these expanded capacities was that we were to become "step-down" units to receive and transmute the incoming new energies down to levels where others could easier assimilate them.

Following are some messages (condensed and combined
from several sessions) that we received while this initiation process was taking place. These messages have never before been
shared with others outside our small group. I hope that they
will provide you some guidance as you approach your own
initiation.

### Message from a Group of Angels
### About the New Energy:

*Yes, you are receiving energy emanations from our Source, for
the first time. We are stepping down these energies and making
them safe for you. These energies are different than anything you
have ever experienced. They will provide spiritual evolvement on a
totally new level, expanded soul growth. You have plans for these
energies and we are coordinating our plans with yours. You have
moved up to our level somewhat so that you can become liaisons
between the two spheres as we come together directly for the first
time.*

*There are few who have reached this level and we grew weary,
waiting and hoping that this evolution might come to pass. We
now know that it has happened and we are so rejoiceful that the
opportunity has been given to lift both you and us to a new level of
enlightenment.*

*The energy itself - the atoms and molecules and physical na-*

*ture of the Light - will pass through your bodies and then out and you will benefit as will others as you balance and bring forth the Light. You have become very important to us and are evolving a close kinship to our group. We have much that we will require of you and we will watch over you and guide you through the various stages. Yes, you have moved greatly and we welcome you into the Hierarchy* (the region of the angels and Masters), *to Shamballa* (an even higher realm, "home" of the Great Ones who embody the Purpose) *and to regions beyond which you have never concerned yourself and still will not concern yourself, except as they touch us, and hence through us, touch you.*

*There are some who cannot comprehend such a deep mission. It requires a special depth of commitment and a complete underlying focus centered in the future. Persons who think only of today can only focus on today. This is not their fault, it is not a conscious decision, yet it is a part of their lives.*

*You have been involved in other things, instructed in other ways - and this is not to say that you are special, but perhaps different, in that you have a commitment that was made before you came onto this planet.*

*Some of you did come from space and spirit and are a "consensus" of other personalities. You came here by choice but did not know that you had made this choice.* (As I found out recently, the choice was made lifetimes ago. More on this in Chapter 7.) *You are understanding now your commitments that have been with you, as if forever.*

*What we need now is a renewed commitment and intention*

*from you. Intentions to become perfect Lights, perfect patterns, as spontaneous combustion for others to allow them to receive into themselves these "fiery" Lights. You will be among a small group from your planet who will be in actual communication with other planets and other peoples. You will be transferring your planetary system into a new system and you will be the pioneers, heralders of the New Age, the new communication, the new Life. Yes, you are a "Stargate Group," working with energies of other planes, transferring them and conforming them to this one.*

### Message from Azriel
### As We Completed the Receiving of Flames:

*In receiving these diplomas you now accept the challenges of the new level. You have graduated and elevated to a new level where your job is to assimilate all of the flames and their meanings and to fuse and blend them within you. You will find that you will be phasing out of old habits and releasing old connections and old crutches as you move into a new phase of your life. There will be many new horizons for you as you embark on a new phase of your consciousness.* (Each of us was told of some new experiences and "jobs" to expect.) *Some of you will be moving out into world events, world communication and world Purposes. You will be moving into relationships that take you to universal levels of communication. We have reached out to you because we believe we can trust you and count on you to help with our Plans and our Purposes. Thank you for your concentrated efforts and for your enduring commitment to the Cause.*

As you can see, these messages dealt mainly with the responsibilities and commitments involved with being a Light

Bearer. This particular initiation is not for everyone (at least not at this time). There are other "lesser" initiations currently being experienced by others, however. As a matter of fact, the entire human population is undergoing some form of initiation. We are, because of the new energy, being lifted - as a planet - onto a new turn of the spiritual spiral. Everyone is affected. No one is left out. Each person, no matter how new to the Path or how far from the Path is being moved an octave higher.

Those whose spiritual natures manifest in the form of simple goodwill and kindness are being initiated into the First Initiation. Those who are beginning to awaken to more soul contact, who sense a desire to "move closer" to that soul nature are being initiated into the Second Initiation. Those who are committed to soul contact and have a conscious desire to sublimate their personality (ego) to this soul nature are taking the Third Initiation. (The Third Initiation is the first one "recognized" by the Hierarchy and is therefore the first of the "higher" initiations, wherein the person makes a *conscious* and deliberate *decision* to move forward spiritually.)

Let us turn our attention now to the topic of initiation and the Masters in whose footsteps we follow and with whose guidance we progress step by step along the Path, living our destinies and creating our future realities.

Chapter 2

# Where Angels Fear To Tread

Perhaps you have noticed that there has been a recent surge in interest in the angel realm. Angel books abound. Everywhere you go, pictures and posters of angels greet you. Angels were always with us, and they have been represented in literature and art since the beginning of time. Why now is there such an upsurge of interest in these heavenly creatures?

The answer, I think, lies in the time, the age in which we live. This is the end of a 2,000 year cycle. At the end of such a cycle, many changes are possible. But because of a special overlap with extra-planetary and universal potentialities (including the availability of new energy to accelerate our affairs) this time is of far greater importance than any other time in the history of mankind. We have been given a special *dispensation* (holy measure) of energy with which to work. This "gift" was not, however, just handed over. We worked for it. All of us, especially those who recognize and respond to the Light, sent forth into the realms of the Hierarchy (the realm or the Masters, angels and Archangels) a plea - *an invocation* - for help. This plea has been responded to and has resulted in a greater closeness with that realm. With the angels closer in our minds (available to us in our meditations and intuitions) this closeness naturally manifests itself in representations in the outer world as well.

## ANGELS AMONG US

In recent years there has been much written about the return of the angels to the earthly plane - to walk among us and to interact with us as "peers." Books such as *The Return of the Bird Tribes* (Ken Carey) and the *11:11* books (Solara Antaris) have predicted their return. Also in the *Alice Bailey Books*, which are transcriptions of instructions given by the Master Djwhal Khul (and are among the more recent sources of ancient esoteric knowledge which I regularly study and trust to be "accurate," the other being the *Urantia Book*), you will find instructions about the return of the Hierarchy and its implications. I have used these sources (especially the *Alice Bailey Books*) to pull together information about the initiations and the return of the Hierarchy and to attempt to *simply* explain it so that it is easier to understand. (The *Alice Bailey Books* are difficult reading and the information in them is scattered. It therefore requires some digging and studying to "make it your own." I hope to simplify this task for newcomers to the books and to present the information that has *current* relevance in all our lives. By doing this, I hope that not only will your understanding of certain esoteric facts be increased, but that you will also be encouraged to read and to study this material for yourself, as it is a great source of spiritual growth and well worth the effort spent.)

## EARTH CHANGES

Those of you familiar with the *11:11* books are aware that Solara, the author, has put forth some amazing and profound declarations. These deal with the changes that are taking place today and her messages about our part in those changes. First, she states that since the time of the Harmonic Conversion on August 16-17, 1987 we have been under a new dispensation of energy (this is the date when the new energies began to reach earth). Because of this divine dispensation, she feels that many of the "earth changes" (floods, earthquakes, volcanoes and every climate change possible all the way up to the planet tipping on its axis and throwing the oceans off onto the land masses and the ocean floors becoming the new land masses) that were predicted will *not* have to happen.

I, for one, was glad to hear that. There have been numerous "earth change" (mostly gloom and doom) predictions, some of which got lots of press (in the book *Mary's Message to the World* by Annie Kirkwood, for instance). Now, I can't say that these things won't still happen (note the number of recent disasters) but it is my belief and the belief of many "optimists" in the spiritual field that these predictions have been superseded by human intervention.

Never in any esoteric material is there *certainty* as to what will happen at any given time in the future. The Masters themselves state often that even they can predict only up to a certain point because evolution is *dynamic* and is *conditioned* by free will. (Note those words.) It allows for the changing of circumstances according to the *united* will of humanity. This is what invocation is all about.

It appears that sufficient numbers of us have consciously held the Light and asked for divine intervention. One of the esoteric "rules" is that when (and if) the invocation is strong enough, the Hierarchy *must* respond. We can all be thankful for two major efforts involved with this. The creation of the Great Invocation (given by the Masters and reproduced in each *Alice Bailey* book) and the World Healing Meditation (created by John Randolph Price in his 1987 book, *The Planetary Commission*) allowed masses of people to come together with a united plea. The creation of a "planetary commission" of Light workers who since 1987 have united their efforts each December 31 at noon Greenwich time, releasing light, love and spiritual energy onto the planet and asking for its healing has indubitably had a profound effect. More recently, the efforts of Solara to unite Light workers to "open the doorway" (secure planetary initiation) by moving the Light to a point of critical mass between the dates given to her as the "available" time span for us to make this spiritual leap - between January 11, 1992 and December 31, 2011 - has also resulted in an unprecedented response by humanity. More than even the Masters could have imagined, we humans have "gotten it together" and have responded to these efforts. This means that more Light workers have been joined the ranks and the "veterans" have been especially diligent in their duties. Through an unexpected show of unity and spiritual focus we have managed to assure the previously only *potential* act of mass initiation and have brought forth help from sources that many of us have only imagined to exist.

The Hierarchy is therefore available to us on a much larger scale than before. Whereas before the Masters and angels were only in touch with a few highly evolved people, today many people are channeling messages from Masters and angels. These great spiritual entities are also available to us through our meditations and our intuitions. In fact, they have always and continue to hope that we will listen to their intuitive whisperings in our spiritual ears.

Mostly what they are saying is "Wake up. You are moving into a new way of being. You must change the way you think and act." As Solara puts it, "We are no longer human beings having a spiritual experience, rather we have become spiritual beings having a human experience." And as Barbara Marciniak, in her recent book, *Bringers of the Dawn*, often repeats, "We are members of the Family of Light." Our job is to free ourselves and others from the hold of duality, to come to understand that there is but one reality, that of Oneness, and to make possible on earth the next manifestation of that Oneness as we progress one step closer to its reality.

The *Bringers of the Dawn* are stated to be space beings who have come to earth from the star constellation of the Pleiadians to bring us a message about how we might help make this happen. Again, the message is essentially "Wake up. Discover who you are. Integrate with all of your soul incarnations and accept both the dark and the light parts. Allow this integration to elevate you to the next level so that you may become a Light beacon for others and make possible a mass rise on the spiral."

## A NEW WAY OF DOING THINGS

As the Alice Bailey book, *Discipleship in the New Age II* explains it, the spiritual growth process of initiation eventually leads to three major accomplishments:

- *Penetration* into the higher realms (contact with the members of Hierarchy).

- *Polarization*, which is an important accomplishment whereby one focuses their attention on their "inner life," (via intuition) to the point where they can hold a meditative state pretty much continuously, alongside, as it were, their normal conscious awareness.

- *Precipitation*, which is the resultant "energy exchange" that occurs when one is able to receive spiritual energy, step it down and spread it to others through actual physical contact (aura to aura) and through service to others as a manifested expression of that energy.

The long term result of these accomplishments is that one who continues to *penetrate* can eventually reach the "Chambers of Shamballa" and receive in sudden intuitive inspirations *direct messages* from this highest source, which have *never before* been available to the reach of the human mind.

These are truly amazing and exciting possibilities. For most of us just connecting for the first time with the Masters, or even with lesser guides, these high contacts represent a great leap in spiritual growth. But again, as I will repeat often, they also represent a bigger responsibility as well. It has often been said that "when the student is ready, the master will appear."

This is really true, but as is pointed out in *Serving Humanity,* the appearance of a Master into one's life depends on a certain kind of readiness, namely that the student has made definite contact with his soul and that the student can hold a *mental* focus.

Much of the work done by the Masters, and therefore by the Master's "disciple" (accepted student) takes place on what is called the mental plane, or the mental realm of consciousness (as opposed to, for instance, the emotional or astral plane.) If one is to be in partnership with the Masters, he must not only prove his dedication and worth, he must also regularly be involved in a mental practice such as meditation that focuses his attention on his *inner* life and allows his conscious self (personality or ego) to benefit from the regular "advice" of his soul (again, received via intuition).

It is also pointed out that the true disciple does not "bother" the Masters with their "petty" human concerns, as Masters are not concerned with the problems of individuals but with the whole of humanity as one. For the same reason, Masters do not seek regular connections to "chit chat." They make contact when there is a reason to do so, usually to lay out the next step of the Plan as it involves the individual and how they might help. Even so, there have been many more "messages" from the Masters recently as evidenced by the growing number of channeled books. One has no way of knowing if all these are "true" messages or if some are illusions - perhaps thoughtforms from the astral plane (the plane of emotion and also illusion, which since the Harmonic Conversion has melded with our third dimension in order that we might now become aware of it and discern for ourselves what is real and what is not real) - or from the person's Higher Self. So even though there are ample "messages" from the Masters, it serves you well to listen to or to read them with an open mind, and be aware that one of the true tests today for mankind is to learn discernment. (This, by the way, goes for my channeled messages, as well. I am never 100% convinced that they are "real," and neither should you be.)

## DUTIES OF THE DISCIPLE

Having said all that, let me now share with you some of the "duties" of those in contact with the Masters. These people are called by various names, but "Light Workers" is the most commonly recognized, and "the New Group of World Servers" is the name given in the *Alice Bailey* books. I will elaborate more on this in Chapter 5, but for now just realize that *you*, by the very fact that you are reading and understanding this book, are a member of this special group.

Not all workers in the Light have at present a direct contact with the Masters, but that is a definite possibility in their lives, as they continue to move quickly on the Path. There are several "ranks" of servers, from those who listen to their intuitive guidance and act upon it with positive intentions for others as well as themselves, to those who get occasional messages and carry our "tasks" as requested, to those who are closely in contact with the Hierarchy on a continuing basis and to whom parts of the Planetary Plan are entrusted.

What, then, does the Hierarchy expect from you if they indeed chose to make contact with you? These are the requests, as noted in the Alice Bailey book, *The Rays and The Initiations:*

- Receive and transmit illumination from your soul.

- Receive inspiration from the Hierarchy and go forth to inspire others.

- Hold the vision of the Plan.

- Act as intermediaries between humanity and the Hierarchy, *receiving light and power* and using these under the influence of love in new fields of service.

As you can see, working with the Masters is serious business. It is not for the meek or lazy. It requires total commitment and dedication, and a willingness to follow one's Path, no matter where it may take you and no matter how much is asked of you.

If you think you are ready for this, the Masters will welcome you into their realm. They stand ready and eager to make new contacts with those who truly desire to help with the great work that is needed today. Remember, it is most likely that your contact will come from the mental plane, through your meditative reflections or perhaps channeled messages. Also, and important to note, is that today, contact with a Master almost always comes within a *group*, not to individual persons. One reason is that the energy of the Hierarchy is now so powerful that it would be dangerous to transmit it to individuals. Another is that the idea of a *group purpose* is something that has become a part of the Plan. (More information on working within a Light Group can be found in Chapter 4.)

On rare occasions the Masters will appear on earth in human form; although they can do this at any time and in times of great need (such as today) they do it more often. Do however, remember too, that *discernment* is a major lesson today, so don't attach yourself indiscriminately to a teacher, thinking that he/she might be a Master. The days of this kind of teaching are basically over, having been replaced by the group work. Most Masters appear only briefly to do a certain job and do not stick around long. As with anything, use your inner guidance to help you discern the truth as you see it.

Humanity as a whole is being served by the assistance of the Masters as they allow us a closer relationship with them. Nonetheless, our lessons are our own to learn, and they will be most often learned within our own minds through soul contact.

Chapter 3

# Initiation: What's That?

I have spoken briefly of the important process of *initiation*. Let me now strive to explain it further. I say "strive" because there is no single simple definition or explanation. It is a process that contains many elements and has many definitions, according to the level of the participant. To give a clear and simple explanation of initiation is perhaps not possible, and perhaps should not be possible. For it is in the seeking that one finds the best explanation. It is the *experience* of initiation, not the definition of it that is needed. Nonetheless, I am going to restate as simply as I can some of the information that I have gleaned about initiation from the *Alice Bailey Books* and from my own experience, to help those who are swiftly coming upon an initiation in their lives.

There was a time not long ago when the highly symbolic language of the older esoteric books - which does present the reader some difficulty in deciphering - served a good purpose. It assured that only those who were dedicated to the Plan would be able to use the information contained in them. But now things are moving so fast that the information is needed by larger numbers of people - the time for understanding is now. I am therefore happy to share with you, the reader, the results of that which I have done for myself, and that which is often suggested in the *Alice Bailey Books* to be done by individuals for their own purposes - and that is to gather together from many books bits and pieces of certain pertinent information which can then be brought together and compared for easier and clearer understanding. These insights provide the foundations of the books and it is with these basic foundation principles that I deal, seeking to make them more accessible to you.

## *INITIATION*

First, what is initiation? As defined in *The Rays and the Initiations*, it is "an expanding series of inclusive recognitions." It is a *group* process whereby each person involved "moves up" to a higher point on the spiritual path. It takes place within each person's own mind, but is precipitated by group action - specifically group invocation and "right thinking."

Previously it was *believed* by initiates that initiation was an individual matter, as indicated by the master/disciple relationship. But now it has been *revealed* that this was an illusion, useful for a time, but now ready to be put to rest. So is it with all spiritual understandings; the information that is revealed at a certain point is given in a manner that will be best understood and accepted by people. Then when a new, higher understanding is possible, more information is given that often renders the old understanding useless and it is then discarded for the new awareness.

Another definition of initiation is "a culminating moment of achievement," when one is finally aware of a new, important spiritual concept, and has gained this awareness by enduring a "crisis" or "test" of his/her dedication to the spiritual life.

Initiation is a "point of tension" or a "fusion of the lights" (intuitions) that allow the initiate to "see deeper and more inclusively."

Initiation is all these things and more. It is, as I have experienced it, a point of *decision* or dedication, a time of aligning oneself ever further with the spiritual self.

Initiation takes place within the mind and heart of the individual but *because of* the work that has been done within a group. Again, it is the group affiliation that is the foundation of initiation. Group work prepares you for the "recognition ceremony" of what has been done and the promise of what is to be done in terms of spiritual growth.

I spoke earlier of some of the "signs" of initiation that I have seen and experienced. The overall experience is a personal *conscious* recognition of one's place and purpose. It can take place, as I have said, with others in a group ceremony or in a hypnosis session, or it can take place when one is alone. My most recent initiation took place within a group setting, but it was later reviewed and other insights given and promises made during a personal, quiet moment. (This was not a dramatic event - in truth, I was sitting at my bathroom vanity, putting on my makeup! But important decisions and commitments were made at this time, perhaps because this was the time when my mind was quiet and "available.")

Once an initiation has been "taken" or experienced, it is not an end, but in reality a beginning, a beginning of new plans and purposes, new responsibilities and new learning experiences. For one "takes" an initiation as he/she is beginning that stretch of the spiritual path, not when he has finished it. So an initiation is a process, not a place; it is a thing one *does,* not gets.

It is also important to remember that initiations, being *processes,* are dynamic. They, in fact, can and do overlap one another. You may be in Initiation 1 in one area of your life and in Initiation 2 in another area. Some days you may live your life in the highest initiation available to you; on other days you may "fall back" to old patterns and attitudes and be "living" a lower initiation. One gets to "take" an initiation a the earliest available point in their growth. Once taken, one strives from then on to live the initiation. This is the process and the plan of initiation. We never "perfect" an initiation, we simply strive to move ever closer to the *revelation* of it within our own lives.

## THE INITIATION PROCESS REVEALED

What does initiation feel like? What does it do in your life? Well, initiation (the process) is first experienced as an *urge to know,* a *seeking.* It is those first "pushes" toward the spiritual path, those first doubts that the "traditional" ways are the only ways. It is the first awakening within one's soul to *conscious* spiritual communication.

Initiation leads to three major accomplishments, as stated earlier: penetration, polarization, and precipitation. Initiation first works to create conflict within one's life and then to help one to deal with that conflict. *Conflict is the test of initiation.*

One begins by seeking and therefore, learning from that which is readily available - books, groups, self-exploration and meditation. Then the initiate learns to "stand on his/her own," to stand fast on the convictions he/she has come to believe, even though these may be counter to "tradition" and may not be understood by many. The initiate learns to distinguish between wishful thinking and intuition, between ambition and service, between his/her own plans and the Path. The initiate consistently moves forward to new, higher understandings, to further contact and increased responsibility to others and to the Plan.

This is done by achieving clarity of mental focus, by practicing the spiritual practices of invocation (asking for help) and evocation (receiving guidance via intuition) and making the meditative state of mind one's natural state. For it is here, within one's own mind that spiritual insights are best to be found. After the books have been read, the classes attended, the group service done, one still must connect with the spiritual sources and *experience the transference of energy*, the spiritual energy that one then begins to *wield* through service to others.

It is no wonder, then, that initiation involves testing and honing of the personality. At first, we are controlled by our personalities. The ego (conscious awareness) is the entire "self." Slowly, though, one becomes aware of the urge to grow, in a spiritual sense. One's soul becomes more active. This starts as the voice of "conscience," whispering in our ears, guiding us to do the right thing. Then as we expand our awareness of spiritual matters and begin to actively seek to listen to the voice, it becomes stronger and begins to "take over" our personalities in the sense that our major *focus of attention* is now within our spiritual life rather than our personal life. This marks the step onto the path of initiation.

## THE ELEVEN INITIATIONS

There are eleven initiations in all and each of us will eventually work through all of them. However, during only five or six of these, at most, will we be in human form. As far as I can discern, many of us will be out of incarnation, freed from "the wheel of karma" by the forth or fifth initiation. Some of us will continue to incarnate as Masters for another few initiations to help others along the Path. Those who move out of Earth service will continue to do other work in extra-planetary realms.

The initiations that concern us then, at this point in our evolution, are really the first three or four, and it is with these that I will deal. Past the fifth and sixth, even the Masters have little knowledge of what is to come. For most of us, it is either the First or Second Initiation that is being faced, and these two are now being made available in group form for the first time. In other words, groups, or masses of people, will all receive these initiations during this current lifetime. A smaller amount of us will be moving into the Third Initiation, the first one to be recognized by the Hierarchy, where our spiritual growth is brought under *conscious* control. Still fewer will be passing into "Master training" and will be recognizing responsibilities and duties as such.

But let us look now to those initiations which concern the majority of us - the first three.

### Initiation 1

This First Initiation is called the "Birth of Christ" and brings with it the understanding of the Christ consciousness. It marks the birth of a new attitude, a new interpretation of life events, where the personality strives to discern Truth over "glamour." (Glamour is, in esoteric terms, the focusing of one's awareness on material or illusionary - from the soul standpoint - things and events.)

In the First Initiation the person begins to think in terms of what is right and what is wrong and to strive to "do the right thing." It is said that at the time of the First Initiation the personality is "at war" with the soul. This is because the person is struggling with his/her first soul awareness and its urges for spiritual rather than personal gains. An example of one going through a First Initiation might be a businessman who begins to see that a purely profit motive that turns its back on the needs of the worker is not one that he any longer wants to pursue.

### Initiation 2

This Second Initiation is called the "Baptism." It is the point at which one realizes that all emotional reactions are based in glamour (illusion) and are therefore, in effect, working against the Self, against integration and soul growth. This is not to say that one should not show emotions, but that one must learn to *control* them, in the esoteric sense. This kind of control does not mean the stoic, unfeeling emotional control of one who is not in touch with his/her emotions, but rather the "relaxed indifference" of one who sees events and circumstances from a bigger perspective, who sees difficulties as learning experiences, conflicts as growth opportunities. This mindset allows a certain emotional distance, where one can *decide* how much psychic energy a situation deserves, vs. being thrown into immediate emotional upheaval as a conditioned response to events and/or thoughts.

The Second Initiation is when we discover that we have control of our lives by having control of our individual reactions. We become masters of our individual worlds. We continue to have conflict between our "lower" (personality) and "higher" (soul) selves, but the first small impulses of the Will nature (the understanding of a purpose to our lives) helps us to move through it toward the higher Path.

Again, remember that these first two initiations are the ones that are available at this time to groups of people - without any real effort on their part. As evolution moves ever upward and forward, initiations are a result.

Yet, for those on the "fast track" evolution moves too slowly. Available for these "seekers" is the Third Initiation.

### Initiation 3

This Initiation is called the Transfiguration, and it marks the first initiation that is recognized by the Hierarchy - to them it is the first true initiation. The Third Initiation is entered into by individuals, one by one, as opposed to mass groups. It is taken deliberately, with full conscious knowledge and commitment. At the time of the Third Initiation a person might be affiliated with a group (as a participant in a meditation group, for example; or perhaps with an association that focuses on group service). However, the idea of group purpose and group service must be a part of the initiate's mindset. He or she must have moved past purely personal motives and must have gained control over his/her emotions, so that the mental focus is now free to move outside one's self, toward others and toward helping others.

At the Third Initiation, the personality becomes *soul infused.* In other words, the soul encompasses the personality to the point that it takes over the thinking processes previously left to personality motives. In some explanations, this is called the "death" of the personality, but in truth, it is more the transformation of the personality to a soul nature.

The Third Initiation is a big step. For it to take place in one's life several criteria must be present. As noted above, the person must have moved from an orientation toward their personal self to a group orientation. This is necessary because the Hierarchy, with whom one begins to have contact with and begins to "work" with at this point, are solely group oriented.

Next, the person must definitely have acquired a *mental focus.* This means that their focus, or awareness, is mainly on things of a mental nature. They must be "thinkers," people who spend a great deal of time on the "mental plane." This mental plane is the "home" of the Hierarchy and it is where the person will "meet" with them. They must begin to be not only familiar with the mental plane but must spend a great deal of time here, to the point where it is "home base" for their awareness.

This means that instead of going around "feeling" your way through situations, you "think" your way through; but again, not in the over-intellectualizing way of the person who is out of touch with feelings, but in the "detached" way of one who has overcome the tyranny of "push button" feelings (when someone "pushes your buttons," you react a certain way). This kind of thinking begins to manifest true *knowledge,* which is the result of intuition coupled with thought; eventually this knowledge is implemented into *service*, motivated by *love*.

At the Third Initiation, the person begins to be guided by the Hierarchal Plan and to for the first time ever to be "in the loop" for new energies *directly* from Shamballa, the source of the Purpose. This new energy source is extremely potent. It is these energies as well as the new energy of the 2,000 year cycle that provide much difficulty for initiates facing the Third Initiation. Prior to this time energies from Shamballa would be too potent for the individual to take. But a "stepping down" of these energies has been allowed so that certain individuals can begin to have contact *for the first time ever* directly with the "master" Masters of Shamballa. Those who receive these energies are receiving the first "answers" to their invocations from this highest source. The initiates of the third degree are being allowed to connect directly to the Shamballa forces, previously only available via the Hierarchy. Again, it is easy to see why such importance is placed at the Third Initiation on commitment and responsibility to the Plan and the Purpose behind the Plan.

At the time of each initiation, the person facing initiation is "tested." Difficulties are placed in the initiate's path to help him/her to gain the necessary strengths to take the initiation at hand. For the First and Second Initiations, these tests consist mainly of personality growth, - the "get yourself together" kinds of things that one associates with self-help or psychology. Emotional cleansing, release of negative psychic energy and forgiveness are key issues.

At the Third Initiation the test is more difficult. It is often seen as the "biggest test of your life." It seems that whatever is most important to you at the time will be up for grabs. The

deepest held desires must be given up, the deepest fears released, the deepest, darkest emotions dealt with. It is a time of
"fine tuning" and "cleaning house" on all levels. It is a time
when all incarnations, all past lives, must be integrated and
accepted. (More in-depth information on "tests" can be found
in Chapter 6.)

These three initiations are the ones that most of us will be
dealing with in this lifetime. There are a few who will be moving to the Fourth or Fifth Initiations, so I will go over these
briefly. But remember, most of us will not be facing these for
some time.

### Initiation 4

This initiation is called the "Renunciation" and it marks
the end of the need for karma in our lives, and the end of our
earthly incarnations. It is the point at which those energies
from Shamballa are controlling the entity (you cannot call one
a "person" at this point). The entity is encapsulated in and
working with pure Purpose. The energy of the Spirit has been
infused and is in direct control. The entity has mastered "har-
mony through conflict" (learned the lessons of life) and has
moved onto higher service, preparing for the "speciality" work
which lies ahead at Initiation 7.

### Initiation 5

This initiation is called the "Revelation" and it marks the point
at which the knowledge and spiritual orientation first begun
in the Fourth Initiation is fully developed. It is when the entity
remains in the *permanent* condition of spiritual control by Spirit.

Remember, initiations are dynamic. One never is permanently "fixed" in a state until this Fifth Initiation. Until then, our focuses and orientations do sometimes "wander." We are *learning* to be spiritual "selves." At the Fifth Initiation we *are* permanently spiritual beings. Never again will we "fall back" to previous levels.

## RESPONSIBILITIES OF THE INITIATE

This gives you a sense of what initiation is about from the standpoint of "achievements." From the standpoint of "responsibilities" there are four:

- *Evocation of new powers* (Being a channel for the energies - not necessarily as a "medium" channeling information, but as a living "transformer" of these electrical, light based impulses, bringing them into your body, stepping them down and returning them to the world via your aura.)

- *Recognition of new fields of service* (Finding your individual Path, discovering your "gift" and giving it.)

- *Freedom of movement within the Hierarchy* (Freedom to contact the Hierarchy, with responsibility to "do your part" to further the Hierarchal Plan in return for this advanced spiritual contact.)

- *New Hierarchal contacts* (New Master affiliations through which you will receive intuitive "instructions" for your part of the work.)

All these things and more are available to each of us, as we all will take every initiation in due time. We will travel every Path and will experience all that there is to experience as we travel the long, long journey back to the Source.

_____

# Chapter 4

# Birds of a Feather:
# Groups and Group Work

We have talked briefly about the need for group work and group affiliation. But what does this really mean? And what does it entail?

There are three reasons that group effort is important in the dynamic process of spiritual growth. First, there are certain energies which, for reasons of safety, can only be "administered" to groups. The Shamballa energy is one such energy. It is normally received by a group, doing group work, because its potency can then be shared and dissipated until the individuals within the group are sufficiently oriented to it to receive it safely.

The second reason that groups are important is that there is a certain kind of invocation, *a parallel response from humanity to the Shamballa evocation,* that must be created to fully anchor these energies and to fully bring ourselves and our planet up to the next spiral on the spiritual Path. This response is called the *antahkarana,* or *"rainbow bridge"* and it can only be built by *group effort.*

## THE ANTAHKARANA

The antahkarana is an "extension of consciousness" and it is created by *group focus.* When a group has a common purpose and focuses its attention sufficiently long and sufficiently hard on that purpose, a "tension" of energies is created. This tension is "sensed" by the Masters who then respond in turn. A tenuous link is set up and a thread of reciprocal energies begins to be built. It is because of this thread that the higher initiations are made possible. *Only a person in the process of taking the Third Initiation can invoke Shamballa and can build the antahkarana. And a person can only do these things with the help of a group.*

Finally, group work is important today because it is through groups, both large and small, that the *planetary antahkarana* will be built. As each individual, with the help of a group, builds their own *individual* and *group* antahkaranas simultaneously, they, in turn, are helping to build a *planetary* antahkarana as well.

Many of you are familiar with esoteric groups, from the ones that advertise in magazines to ones who hold secret ceremonies where esoteric symbolism prevails. Such groups have always been important, holding the "mysteries" intact and preventing them from being lost. Today many esoteric teachings are no longer hidden. The time has come when they can be revealed to all. The new work of groups today is not so much to preserve the mysteries as it is to allow for new contact with higher sources - via the antahkarana.

As evolution moves forward, new methods and new experiences are gained. At one point there was no Hierarchy. But through evolution and through the spiritual growth of humans through countless incarnations (no matter how small in comparison to today's), we are now at the point where we not only have a Hierarchy that both helps and is helped by humanity, we also have direct contact with even higher energies. This contact necessitated a totally new line of communication. Therefore, the pattern for an antahkarana came into being, and now it is being created "from scratch," as it were, by those on earth today who are working on the Third Initiation or higher. (You do not need to have received the Third Initiation Ceremony to be working on the Third Initiation. Indeed, the ceremony may come after you have been working in the energies of this initiation for some time. It is once the time of the Third Initiation testing is complete, or is nearing completion, that you experience the ceremony.)

It is the successful building of the planetary antahkarana that assures our elevation to the next turn of the evolutionary spiral. This is what the *11:11* ceremonies were all about. It is what the various angel messages are about. Group invocation of a new and potent type has been made possible by the building of this spiritual "rainbow bridge." (The "rainbow" pertains to the colors of the energy "rays" that make up the antahkarana. All seven of such ray energies are present.)

Another way to explain the antahkarana, as mentioned in *The Rays and the Initiations,* is to say that it is a "thread of consciousness which embodies the *response* of one's consciousness *to* steadily expanding spiritual contacts." A second definition is that it is "the process of *projecting consciously* the triple energies of the personality (as impulsed by the soul) *across a gap.*"

This last definition requires some further explanation. Note first that in this definition the antahkarana is a projecting agent, whereas in the previous definition it is a receiving agent. In fact, it is both. The antahkarana is the connecting link between mankind and the Shamballa energies, both "coming" and "going." Note, then, the words "across a gap." This energy link-up must reach across a gap in the communication line.

Why is that? One possibility is that the whole idea behind building the antahkarana is to show sufficient *desire* for contact. We have been given all the "freebie" spiritual contacts we will get; the time for *unconscious* spiritual evolution is over. From now on, we must consciously desire and work for our spiritual growth. It is neither given nor forced on us past the point of the Second Initiation. From here on out, free will rules our spiritual growth, just as it rules our individual lives.

One thing that I have always taught about the emotion of desire is that it is an energy that acts as a spark plug to "jump start" our actions, to get us moving in the direction of our intentions. Perhaps, here, too, as we are building the three types of antahkaranas - individual, group and planetary - we need to "jump start" our intentions. For if there is not sufficient desire, the antahkarana cannot be built. If there is not a conscious intention and focus on the effort, it will fail. Perhaps the Masters are "testing" us yet again by leaving a gap between us and them, a gap that can only be jumped across by desire that is strong and sure of this spiritual contact.

If so, this test is part of the Plan and it has a Purpose that will prove perfect and true in the end. But for many of us, it has meant yet another obstacle to overcome, yet another stretch of our resources, yet another close call as we worked and wondered, "Will we make it? Will we be able to build the planetary antahkarana in time? Or will we be doomed to another 2,000 year cycle before the opportunity returns again to make this vital contact?"

Fortunately, I believe we have made it. My "sources" and the consensus of many other optimists in the esoteric field indicate that we have indeed, made the *turning point.* We, in numbers large and small, in group efforts, both individually and "piggybacked" to other group efforts, did send out the invocation with the strength required. We have, with our personal and group intentions and desires and *mental focus,* created that thread of energy that was energized and potent enough to jump across the gap.

That does not mean, however, that we are done. What it means is that our energy has been "registered" by Shamballa. We are officially "recognized." Shamballa is aware of our efforts and our success. However, it waits for our fuller development and activation of the planetary antahkarana to really extend to us it's full "attention." As we continue to build the thread, enlarging and strengthening it, our contact will grow ever stronger. We will be permitted deeper into the "Chambers of Shamballa," and have to us, just as we currently do from Hierarchy, help and guidance on an even bigger and grander scale. We will extend our reach and our connection beyond anything now possible, into extra-planetary realms and to the realms of the Spirit itself.

Sounds exciting, doesn't it? Indeed, it is exciting, and it is a challenge that many of us are ready for. In numbers never before possible, we are building - and strengthening - the antahkarana. Light Groups of all kinds, in all nations, are individually and collectively making truly possible the first direct contacts with Shamballa.

## BUILDING THE ANTAHKARANA

How exactly, is this "thread of consciousness" built? It is built through and from its source - mental energy.

The antahkarana is, when all is said and done, a form of *mental energy*; that is why a mental focus is so necessary in its formation. Let's first look a bit more closely at what this thread is made of, and then at how one can begin to build it.

The antahkarana is, in fact, a threefold thread. It is made of three parts, or kinds, of mental energy:

• The *sutratma*, or life force thread.

• The *consciousness* thread itself.

• The *creative* thread, the energy or force behind creativity.

These three threads are the energy that, with conscious focus and intention, can move across the gap between our current spiritual reality and that which lies ahead.

These threads are strengthened by several factors. Knowledge is one. As we increase our awareness and knowledge, we increase the energy of the creative thread. Then we move forward with our emotional growth and begin to fuse our personalities and our souls, we increase the consciousness thread, moving from an emotional focus to a mental focus. When this happens the energy available from the life force thread is increased, and we now become "clearer channels" for its Light.

As you might guess from the above, the major work of

making the initial connection with the higher spiritual energy sources - via the antahkarana - is done between the Second and Third Initiations.

How does this happen? What can you, the aspiring initiate of the third degree, do to assure that you successfully build your own antahkarana? First, remember that building of the antahkarana is a group process. You must attach yourself to a group of like minded people and with mutual protection and guidance, move forward as a unit.

I will get into group process in a moment, but first let me list for you four stages of the antahkarana building process:

- *Intention* - As mentioned earlier, intention is a real force. It is more than a deciding type of thinking process or a determination. It is a *holding of focus of one's mental energy* on a certain purpose. It is a time of the "gathering of one's forces" prior to the next step in the building process.

- *Visualization* - Visualization has long been a part of the esoteric student's life. However, this picture forming mind exercise has a more potent role in this process. Visualization involves an activating, "stepping up" process whereby the *force* of mental energy is actually increased. Through visualization, one can step up the mental energies to the point that they can *move toward* the waiting point of tension. When this happens, there is an "activity" and "organization" of the mental energy being focused. The energy is then ready for its release and transference into the next stage of development.

- *Projection* - This is the deliberate "throwing out" of the visualized mental energy into the arena of the higher spiritual energies. It is the time when the thought, the visual image, and the desired intention is let go, *released*, to do its work. Projection requires both a build-up of energy/force to a critical point, and then the knowledge of when and how to properly release it. It requires the use of the *Will energy*, that energy which is related to the Shamballa forces, which has steadily been increasing in the mind of the individual. This Will energy only becomes available in the life of a person when the soul has begun to control one's daily activities.

Next in this process is the use of a *Word of Power*, but in truth, it can be more accurately called a *thought of power* for it is not the sound of the word itself but their spiritual meaning that is important. When the full understanding and acceptance of the meaning of the word(s) of power are a part of the person's daily consciousness, then the third stage of building the antahkarana is complete. The word or thought of power is different for each of the seven rays of life energy. These words of power are to be used as *affirmations* or *assertations* of realizations within one's ever expanding mind. The words of power themselves are non-translatable so the following are the meanings of the words of power for each of the seven rays, to be *mentally* and *silently* said at the time of projection:

Ray One: *I Assert the Fact.*

Ray Two: *I See the Greatest Light.*

Ray Three: *Purpose Itself Am I.*

Ray Four: *Two Merge With One.*

Ray Five: *Three Minds Unite.*

Ray Six: *The Highest Light Controls.*

Ray Seven: *The Highest and the Lowest Meet.*

Obviously, there is much behind these words, which we will not go into in this book. If you are nearing the point needing to use these words, you should be reading the Alice Bailey texts and gathering up the information that you need, for each person's focus will be different according to the ray type that they are, and part of the antahkarana building process is for one to discern his/her own ray type and how best to use one's words of power.

- *Invocation and Evocation* - When the visualization and intended thought are projected the Will of the higher sources is evoked, and the "gap" is closed. Then the antahkarana is fully activated. (This full activation will not take place until the Fourth Initiation. Until then, one is working to strengthen the threefold thread.)

Once, however, this gap has been crossed, no matter how tentatively, the first *direct* contacts with the sources of Shamballa are made and the person moves up a rung on the spiritual spiral in both ability and responsibility. For the obvious reasons, this does not take place until the initiate's life is clearly focused within the soul and service is his/her main intention (and not selfish desire).

Now, what does all this mean, really? As a person who has

experienced some of the above steps, I can perhaps put your mind to rest by first saying that much of this work can, and often does, go on without full, conscious deliberate effort. In other words, the work of building the antahkarana may be well on its way before you consciously and fully realize that you are taking part in it, so don't worry if you feel that you haven't even begun. You probably have and just don't know it. Remember, the First and Second Initiations do not require full conscious knowledge; only at the point of the Third Initiation is this necessary. So, in other words, like those in my Group, you, too, may have been taking part in this process long before you knew. We did not sit down one day and say, "Let's build an antahkarana." We didn't even know the term at the time. But we were responsive to our Group Master's suggestions. We were consciously desirous of continuous spiritual growth. We did listen to and follow our intuitive urges which led us to do things that moved us in these directions and that opened our awareness to new contacts and to new ways of communicating. It was only after all of this happened, and after our Initiation Ceremony that I came across the teachings about the antahkarana.

This seems to be a standard practice in my intuitive life. Because I am, even after all this, still somewhat of a "doubting Thomas," I find that corroboration of "messages" or events, for me, most often comes after the fact, perhaps to more easily convince my skeptical side. After we had had a year or so of messages about a new way of communicating, new and greater sources to become available to us, new and greater responsibilities, we did receive the "promised" rewards (also ending, thankfully, a time of great testing for us all.) A totally new way of channeling became evident, and it seemed that the old method was to be put aside. New and higher sources were contacted and began contacting us. New responsibilities and jobs were given. We all moved to a higher rung on our individual spirals, and our Group work soon appeared to be done, as we began receiving messages about a parting of the ways, which did occur about a year later.

The point is, though, that we did not set out to take part in a structured, four step antahkarana-building process. These four steps were naturally enfolded into our Group work. They *naturally* took place as we went about our Group business.

## GROUP WORK

This brings us to an important point about groups. To be a Light Group and to contribute to the cause of bringing Light to the world and ensuring spiritual growth and evolvement of every person, a Light Group must embody certain aspects. While there is no specific standard set of rules for Light Groups, and no specific way a Group must run, there are certain necessary *functions* that the Group must provide in order to be an *active participant* in the world Work.

If you belong to a Light Group, your efforts are part of this worldwide plan, whether you were aware of it or not. Any time Light is put out, the invocation is strengthened. But with *conscious purpose of mind* and *intention* and *focus* on the specific goal, such effects are dramatically enhanced. All Light Groups are members of the New Group of World Servers or the Planetary Commission or the Light Workers, as such groups are commonly called. You need no membership card, no identification except that of you own Light shining forward. However, in this time of great change and need, it is useful for all

Light Workers to stand up and be counted, to take part consciously and deliberately in the world Work.

If you want to be a part of this larger purpose, you and your Light Group should be working to make contact with a Master and to discern your individual and group service. You must have a *group purpose* and this group purpose must take precedence over individual personality differences, interpersonal conflicts and the like. There must be a *group unit* built and a *group energy* formed. This is not an easy task, as we humans tend to become easily distracted by our own personal problems and desires. It is a rare group that can stay together and hold a purpose long enough to create a group energy and group purpose, to build a group (and thereby, also, individual) antahkarana(s), and to be assigned a group Master to guide the group and direct their service efforts.

I have been involved in three different Light Groups, and only one has had the tenacity to withstand all these challenges. The other two, newer and still experiencing "growing pains" are moving ahead but seem to lack either the group purpose or the unconditional acceptance to overcome the inevitable personality conflicts. This is not said to find fault, but to illustrate the difficulty involved in moving forward *together, as a group,* on a determined Path.

There are endless ways to run a group or association, and Light Groups are no different. But I think it might be useful to share with you some of the methods that we used in our first group, the most longstanding and successful, from the standpoint of movement and tangible accomplishment. This group began with four or five members as a "discussion group," discussing New Age books, and it quickly evolved into much more. Over the seven years that we were together, we built up to a dozen members, with seven being the average number. By the end, however, there were but three of us to take part in the Initiation Ceremony.

I feel that we were successful in that we stayed together despite personality conflicts, despite occasional differences of opinion over the direction of the Group, and despite the growing time constraints on all members, making it difficult at times to set aside the necessary time allotment for the weekly meetings. Dedication was a key factor here, for of the three of us who stuck it out the longest, there were very few occasions when we missed a meeting, having made it a big priority in our lives, in contrast to a "diversion" or casual commitment. Also, we put the solidarity of the Group, the Group integrity, above all else, and on many occasions set aside our own interpersonal conflicts to keep the Group together.

Another factor that is important, I think, for such a Group to survive and flourish is a sense of common purpose. As noted earlier, this sense of purpose gave our group a focus that we could *as a unit* focus upon. We all had our personal desires, our personal goals, and these were dealt with in turn. But as time went by, and our spiritual growth continued, our visualizations and meditations about personal goals lessened and our attention became more strongly focused on the group purpose. Our group purpose had early on been determined to be world healing, so each meeting incorporated some world healing aspect.

We also recognized the need for group unity and acceptance. When different people of different backgrounds get together, there are bound to be problems and personality conflicts. We spent much time in the early months and years working on exercises and meditations to "bond" us as a group. Some of these were as simple as each person in the group going around in a circle, telling each of the others what we loved about them. Other times we brought in exercises from a book we had read. (There are numerous such activities available in books, so I will not elaborate on these. Some searching at the bookstore should provide your group with enough exercises to keep you busy and result in the bonding needed.) Sometimes we gave healing "treatments" to one another, or did experiments with stones or crystals. These early days were filled with much personal conversation and fun, yet we always got down to business, thanks to our resident "taskmaster."

For a group to succeed, a Light Group or any other kind, there does need to be some sort of structure, some guidelines to follow. Otherwise, as I'm sure you have experienced, things can fall into chaos or can simply not move forward. We did not have a "leader" per say in our Group, but we did have, as I mentioned, a person who had the necessary managerial and personal skills to move us toward a specific goal each meeting. She took upon herself (probably because no one else would) the unenviable task of keeping us on target, planning an informal agenda, and making sure that we accomplished certain objectives each meeting, despite our tendency to prolong the chit-chat, especially when the group was larger. Without this discipline, we may never have accomplished all that we did. As an extra bonus, this person was our unofficial "transcriber." Because of her tireless work I was able to include in this book excerpts from some of the messages that were received.

Not every group will have such a person, but some accommodations must be made for assuring that your group does not fall apart because of a lack of continuity and structure. One of the two later groups I mentioned uses a rotating method of putting the person whose home is the meeting place in charge of that meeting's agenda. This works well if everyone will do their part when it is their turn.

Finally, I think I should mention that our original group made a decision to be a "closed" group, in that when we selected our participants, we pretty much stuck with them and did not invite people to "drop in." As the years went by, we did, of course, have members who came and went, but we asked that a new member be pretty much dedicated to the group and make a commitment to it. Other groups are more "open" in that they hold a meeting and whoever shows up, friends of friends, or even strangers, are welcome. The problem with this is that it is more difficult to hold a group purpose, to create a group energy and to move forward as a unit when the group members keep changing. That is not to say that one should not run their Group that way, but it is simply something to think about.

## GROUP FORMAT

Having given you these preliminary insights about how we ran our Light Group, I think it might now be useful for you if I share with you some of the specific exercises and meditations that we used in the early days. I often encourage my *Miracles of the Mind* class students to form their own Groups, especially those having finished *Miracles 2,* the "advanced" class. They often ask how to go about doing that and I find that this informal agenda is helpful to them, not to be a set pattern to follow, but to simply provide some suggestions from which they can then begin to formulate their own ideas for their group agenda.

I hope that these ideas will prove useful to you as well. My own particular group has a format like this:

- Lord's Prayer
- World Healing Meditation
- Affirmations
- Personal Chakra Balancing
- Chakras of the Earth Balancing
- One Focus Meditation for Goals
- Open Focus Meditation for Receiving Intuitions

We always started with the Lord's Prayer because we felt that it aligned us with our Source. We took very seriously the words "Thy Will be done." What we did in our group was to ask to be supplements for accomplishing the Will, the Purpose of God on earth. When we visualized and affirmed our goals for world healing, or whatever else, we did so with the stipulation that if the will of God was different from ours, we would defer to His will. However, our general consensus of opinion was that as humans we were meant to attempt to help ourselves, and that sending out our meditations was an important part of the evolutionary process in which we found ourselves at that time.

The following World Healing Meditation is a beautiful meditation that is repeated by many different groups. It first appeared in the book *The Planetary Commission*, by John Randolph Price (The Quartus Foundation, Publisher) and is reprinted with permission here. This meditation seems to strike a chord in many people, and they intuitively feel that it is a powerful tool for accomplishing world healing. Our Light Group used this meditation; perhaps you will find it appropriate for your group, too. I will give you the meditation here and afterwards I will add a few comments about it.

## WORLD HEALING MEDITATION

*In the beginning*
*In the beginning God.*
*In the beginning God created the heaven and the earth.*
*And God said let there be Light; and there was Light.*

*Now is the time of the new beginning.*
*I am a co-creator with God, and it is a new heaven that comes,*
*As the Good Will of God is expressed on Earth through me.*
*It is the kingdom of Light, Love, Peace and Understanding.*
*And I am doing my part to reveal its Reality.*

*I begin with me.*
*I am a living Soul and the spirit of God dwells in me, as me.*
*I and the Father are one, and all that the Father has is mine.*
*In truth, I am the Christ of God.*

*What is true of me is true of everyone,*
*    for God is all and all is God.*
*I see only the Spirit of God in every soul.*
*And to every man, woman and child on Earth I say:*

*I love you, for you are me. You are my Holy Self.*

*I now open my heart,*
*And let the pure essence of Unconditional Love pour out.*
*I see it as a Golden Light radiating from the center*
*    of my being,*
*And I feel its Divine Vibration in and through me,*
*    above and below me.*

*I am one with the Light.*
*I am filled with the Light.*
*I am illumed by the Light.*
*I am the Light of the world.*

*With purpose of mind, I send forth the Light.*
*I let the radiance go before me to join the other Lights.*
*I know this is happening all over the world at this moment.*
*I see the Merging Lights.*
*There is now one Light. We are the Light of the world.*

*The Light of Love, Peace and Understanding is moving.*
*It flows across the face of the Earth,*
*Touching and illuminating every soul*
*    in the shadow of the Illusion.*
*And where there was darkness,*
*    there is now the Light of Reality.*

*And the radiance grows, permeating,*
*    saturating every form of life.*
*There is only the vibration of one Perfect Life now.*
*All the kingdoms of the Earth respond,*

*And the planet is alive with Light and Love.*

*There is total Oneness,*
*And in this Oneness we speak the Word.*
*Let the sense of separation be dissolved.*
*Let mankind be returned to Godkind.*

*Let peace come forth from every mind.*
*Let love flow forth from every heart.*
*Let forgiveness reign in every soul.*
*Let understanding be the common bond.*

*And now from the Light of the world,*
*The One Presence and Power of the Universe responds.*
*The Activity of God is healing*
    *and harmonizing Planet Earth.*
*Omnipotence is made manifest.*

*I am seeing the salvation of the planet*
    *before my very eyes,*
*As all false beliefs and error patterns are dissolved.*
*The sense of separation is no more;*
*The healing has taken place,*
    *and the world is restored to sanity.*

*This is the beginning of peace on Earth*
    *and Good Will toward all,*
*As Love flows forth from every heart,*
*Forgiveness reigns in every soul,*

*And all hearts and minds are one*
    *in perfect understanding.*
*It is done. And it is so.*

This meditation is without a doubt one of the most beautiful and useful meditations for world healing that you might hope to find. It was given to John Randolph Price to disseminate to the world, and along with the *Great Invocation* is one of the two recent "gifts" from Hierarchy that have the power to stimulate major changes on our planet. For this reason, people all over the world get together (physically and spiritually) each New Year's eve (December 31) at 12:00 noon Greenwich time to release Love, Light and Spiritual Energy onto the planet by speaking this Meditation.

Note in the third section of the Meditation the words "I and the Father are one, and all that the father has is mine. In truth, I am the Christ of God." This passage is saying that all of us, as parts of God, and someday returning to God, are creators in our own way. It represents a potential for creativity and unfoldment that we are just beginning to manifest.

As we repeat this Meditation with awareness and faith we are, in fact, creators as we manifest the healing of our planet through the use of our collective visualization and invocation. So let me now share with you some imagery that I personally use with this Meditation, to illustrate how you can enhance your own meditations (this one or any other) by overlapping meditation and visualization together.

Starting in the fifth segment of the World Healing Meditation (I now open my heart and let the pure essence of Unconditional Love pour out...) I visualize the Golden Light of Unconditional Love as it radiates from me, filling me and illuminating me. Then I visualize sending it forth (I picture this as a sort of laser beam emanating from my forehead), seeing the Lights from other Light Workers joining mine.

I visualize as clearly as I can this Light flowing across the earth, over the land, saturating it with loving energy.

Then I visualize the hands of God (as large hands of White Light energy) as they reach around the entire earth, gently holding it, and radiating to the earth this loving energy.

Finally at the end of the meditation I imagine love flowing forth from people as they walk and talk with one another. I imagine them reaching out to hug one another, saying that all misunderstandings are gone. I see all the people of the earth, and the earth itself, radiating in the loving energy.

In this way, I add more power, more energy, to the meditation, sending it out with positive purpose, with loving intentions, hoping and believing that it does help bring the world closer to peace, love and understanding.

Everyone in our group probably visualized the Meditation a little bit differently, but the intentions are all the same - the healing and saving of planet, and ourselves. It is the group *intent*, I believe, and not the individual pictures that matter.

Now to go on to the next part of our Light Group format. We followed the World Healing Meditation with several positive affirmations:

- Love is the answer to all.

- I invoke the Light of Christ within.

- I am a clear and perfect channel for the Light.

- I now release anything and everything that are not a part of my Divine Plan.

- I now let go and let the Divine Plan of my life unfold.

Then we visualized our *chakras* (body energy centers) "opening," using a Chakra Energy Exercise. (One such exercise can be found in my book, *Tools for Transformation.* I also have an audiotape available which contains several different chakra exercises. See the back of this book.)

If you are new to chakra meditations, you may not "feel" anything at first; that is OK. With time, you will open the chakras. In truth, opening one's chakras is a process that should be done very carefully and not before one is ready - meaning that you have cleared up any old emotional issues that are keeping you focused primarily on yourself. Only when you have "freed up" your energies by moving your attention from yourself can you gain real success in opening the chakras, because to do so earlier would only add energy to the negatives within you, which could result in physical illness. In this way your mind is wise and protective and you should not try to "override" such protective measures by excessive or premature attention to chakra opening. (For this very reason, my Chakra Awakening Tape contains both "beginner" and "advanced" exercises.)

Next we visualized the earth as having chakras, so that we could imagine it "opening" up to the positive energy of the universe as well. (It is interesting to note that we created this exercise long before we realized its real Truth - see Chapter 8.) This Earth Chakra Energy Exercise was a group effort, first thought of by two of our members and then added to by the rest. I think it turned out to be a worthwhile and very effective visualization, and I am pleased share it with you:

## EARTH CHAKRA ENERGY EXERCISE

Visualize the chakras of the "body" of the planet. The first chakra is the root chakra which represents *all living things*. Hold your attention on this chakra and imagine it "opening" to allow a free flow of universal energy through it.

Next, visualize the second chakra of the earth, the sexual chakra, representing the *life force*. Hold your attention there until you sense a "movement" or opening here.

Then visualize the third chakra of the earth, the solar plexus chakra, representing the *core of the earth*. Hold your attention here and imagine this chakra opening.

Next imagine the fourth chakra of the earth, the heart chakra, representing *the land*. Hold your attention on this chakra until it opens.

Now imagine the fifth chakra of the earth, the throat chakra, representing *the people* of the earth. Hold your attention on this chakra until it opens.

Go on to imagine the sixth earth chakra, the "third eye," representing the *Higher Self* of man. Hold your attention here until this earth chakra opens.

Finally, visualize the seventh earth chakra, the crown chakra, representing *man's conception of heaven*. Hold your attention here and imagine this chakra opening.

The use of such visualizations can help you and your group to move higher on your spiritual path. They can also help the earth to become more "opened" to the free flow of universal energy, and to be released from any buildup of negative ener-

gies caused by the negative thought patterns, hates and preju-
dices that we have lived with for so long.

Having done the Earth Chakra Energy Exercise, our group
then had a period of one focused meditation to send forth
"requests" for assistance in several areas. Requests for world
healing included mentioning any trouble spots in the world
(sometimes we discussed these aloud just prior to the meditation time.) We also added any personal healing requests for
ourselves, our loved ones, or others whom we knew who needed
healing, in the physical sense or otherwise. (Sometimes at this
point we would add requests for the homeless, AIDS patients,
or any other groups who might need healing energies.)

We sometimes also added our own personal requests for
things which we hoped would be on our path; however we did
not make this the central focus of our group.

Finally, we sat quietly in meditation, allowing ourselves to
experience the quiet stillness and receptivity necessary to receive intuitive messages. We listened for subconscious messages,
thoughts or ideas that might drift to the surface of our
consciousnesses. These quiet messages often led us to the next
step on our Divine Path, and they proved to be valuable sources
of personal and group wisdom.

We felt that meditating in a group added a special effec-
tiveness that we did not get when we meditated alone. It also
allowed us to use others as sounding boards, as we discussed
and refined in our own minds the ideas and inspirations that
surfaced as we tuned into our intuitive selves.

Chapter 5

# At Your Service

As stated many times in this book, you, too, are members of a Light Group, simply by the fact that you do work in the Light, whether that work is being done within a smaller, structured Light Group like the one just mentioned, or within the overall loosely connected Light Group worldwide network whose Light combines to do the World Work. In truth, all who work in the Light at all are connected to this larger World Group, either consciously or unconsciously.

This membership has its privileges - and its duties. The privileges are contact with higher sources, increased energy available for both personal and world work, and accelerated spiritual growth.

## SPIRITUAL REWARDS

I might mention briefly - as I have so far tended to focus on the responsibilities and not the rewards of initiation - that once the tests that precede each initiation are passed, one is more than amply rewarded for these efforts. An increase in contact and communication through intuition is gained at the First and Second Initiation stages, along with extra energy for visualization, affirmations and "programming" of personal goals. At the Third Initiation stage, the contacts are more direct and intuitive knowledge dramatically increased, as well as the "power" one can wield through visualization, thought projection, and affirmations. Also, there is an increase in other psychic energies, such as new or increased abilities to heal, see auras, etc, which began to blossom during the previous two stages. Finally, there is the sense of inner peace and connectedness that one gets from knowing that you are on your true Path and that you are giving your own special "gift" to the world. We will go more in-depth into tests and rewards in the next chapter. For now, let's look at the real emphasis of spiritual growth - the progressive movement and orientation toward service.

## SERVICE AND THE "DUAL LIFE"

As you reach into the higher spiritual realms, you will find your focus moving away from yourself and outward, toward others. Your mind's attention will no longer be needed to be placed solely on your self and your daily needs and desires. These will have been taken care of as you progressed through Initiations 1 and 2. You will find your thoughts and your energies directed toward your "destiny," your Path. You will begin to have an intense interest in discovering your destiny, being on your Path and giving your gift.

The Masters will be there to work with you to help you to

find your Path, to find ways to give your gift. Opportunities will open up to you to serve. All you have to do to get them is to be open to the intuitive messages being transmitted to you.

As you progress on your spiritual growth, you will discover the need to live "the dual life"- first the outer, traditional life of worker, family member etc, and then the "inner life" of the subjective, contemplating soul. The task that lies ahead of us all is to regain on a conscious level all that has been gained and stored up at a soul level through our numerous incarnations. Remember, after the Third Initiation, none of us, except those who return as Masters to help the upcoming groups, will be incarnate. We will be done with the need for karma, but not with the need for the lessons that karma taught us. Now we must begin to bring that knowledge to the surface. Many of us will experience past life recall, even recall of lives in other forms. But much of this growth and karma release will take place *through the act of service.*

It is often when you help others that you help yourself. Service means doing something for others. Granted, we all give and receive "service" every day. Many jobs today are "service" jobs - food service, transportation, information gathering and dissemination, consultation, etc. We pay to have things done for us; we pay for services. But this idea of service is different. The difference lies in the *intention.*

When you give or receive service for pay, you are engaging in commerce. When you give service freely, and with no intention of repayment, you are engaging in community commitment. You are "giving up" for the good of the whole.

Most of us want to feel valuable, to "do something important." The tendency to be altruistic, to help others simply for the sake of helping, is a common human trait that psychologists say evolved as an innate, natural tendency, possibly as a self-preservation tool. Contributing to the betterment of the world helps us all. It helps us survive as a species.

Service for the good of the whole is not only useful for the self-preservation of our species, it is useful for the ongoing processes of transformation and spiritual evolution. Service to others is, in fact, key to spiritual growth. Unselfish service to another moves your focus for the first time totally away from yourself. It allows you the freedom to act solely from your spiritual self, your soul self, the self that is committed to loving, sharing and caring. By removing the focus from the purely "selfish" interests of your personality or ego, you can give more and give more sincerely.

## YOUR GIFT

We all have something to give. Each of us come to the world with some unique "gift" to share. This "gift" is our own little piece of the truth, our unique view of the world, our own understanding of the universal plan. By sharing our gift, we broaden the perspectives of the world for others. We allow them to see things that they would not see, understand things that they would not understand.

When you engage in service to others, you give a twofold gift. You first of all give the gift of the service itself, the good deed that you do. Secondly, and perhaps even more importantly, you give the gift of positive interaction between yourself and others. This positive human interaction sets up a pattern of positive thoughts and behaviors that can greatly influence our future evolution.

The attitude of service is the keynote of the initiated disciple (or *initiate*). This person who has reached the Third Initiation is now pledged to do the group work and to work with Hierarchy toward the implementation of the Plan. The initiate is expected to:

- Serve humanity.

- Cooperate with the Plan.

- Live and work by following his/her soul guidance or intuition.

- Discover his/her own unique work (gift) and give it with love.

## YOU ARE HERE FOR A PURPOSE

How does one do these things? How does one discover the meaning and purpose of his own life?

Most of us have asked ourselves such questions at some point or another. As a person consciously moving forward on your spiritual path, you have probably spent more time than most people contemplating the latter question. We humans seem to have an innate need for purpose in our lives. Most of us aren't satisfied believing that life just is, that you live the best you can, and then you die. We look for a reason behind it all. Deep inside, most of us feel that there must be more to life than simple existence.

If you look within, you will find that there is a reason, a purpose for your existence on earth. Each of us is part of the Divine Plan, a part of the tapestry of life. Each life is unique. Each life adds a special, individual richness to the tapestry. Each of us as an individual is but one small thread in the tapestry; yet each and every thread has a special place, a special function. No life is insignificant; no life is unimportant. Each has its responsibility to the whole.

We each have a purpose and a destiny that we can help create. We can choose to float aimlessly along, and allow circumstances to shape our destinies, or we can take charge of our destinies by discovering and living our true purpose. The choice is individual. Each person alone must choose whether or not he will follow his unique path or will allow circumstances to move him forward.

By choosing to take control of your life and to *consciously* follow your Path, you take the "high road" or "fast track" to spiritual growth. You move forward quickly and grow much in one lifetime. If you chose to take the slow and steady path, that is fine, too. But it may be another 2,000 year cycle before you get another opportunity to move to the next spiritual level. That is why the era we live in today is so important. We have an unprecedented opportunity to move forward to a new way of being, a to new spiritual spiral - if we so choose.

## DISCOVERING YOUR PURPOSE IN LIFE

There is a purpose, a meaning to your life. You can discover your "gift" and find the best ways to give it;  you can be of service to your fellow humans and thereby grow on your spiritual path.

Simply ask and you shall find the way. If you truly desire to know your purpose and are willing to go where it directs you - if you intend to live the life of service - then you will surely find your Path. You can start by first meditating on the question of your life's purpose, reflecting on it, truly *desiring* an answer.

Then listen to your intuition. Your intuition will guide you toward your ideals, toward your own unique path in life, where you can be of service to others, and grow spiritually. Learn to recognize your own "intuition signals" and follow up on true intuitions. The more you follow your intuitions, the more your inner self will present them to you.

Often we are so wrapped up in the desire to "do something," to "make things happen" that we forget to let our inner guidance direct us. We can go off on the wrong track many times before we finally get frustrated and in desperation say, "*I* don't know what I'm supposed to do. Please God, tell me and I'll do it." Then, once we begin *listening,* we begin to be directed by our intuition.

## EVALUATING INTUITION

How can you tell when that "inner voice" is really your intuition speaking, and not "wishful thinking"? How can you tell that it is a message from you Higher self or soul and not just a stray thought?

True intuitive messages have something special about them, but what exactly that is you must decide for yourself as it is different for each person. You do, however, have special intuition "cues" that can be discerned through quiet reflection. The best way to begin noticing and recognizing these cues is to keep an intuition log. Write down each time that you get a feeling or hunch that you feel might be intuitive. Write down, also, everything that you feel or sense at that same time, paying special attention to subtle inner reactions such as "butterflies" in the stomach, a subtle smell or change in mental perception - increased or decreased clarity, a "knowingness" or sense of urgency. Look also for differences in thought "transmission." Perhaps the message sounds different in tone, or is delivered in second person rather than first person ("You should do this" vs. "I think I should do this"). Perhaps the message repeats itself (three times is often common) or is "stronger" than normal thoughts or urges. Be open to any small nuances or differences. Intuitions are both fleeting and quiet. They come as the beating of butterfly wings, not as the clanging of a bell.

Also use your dreams, your direct link to your subconscious, to help you discover your Path in life. Ask for dreams that lead you to an understanding of your life's plan and purpose.

Discerning subtle intuitive messages and understanding dreams is not a simple task. It requires a steady focus of attention to the "inner life." And that is exactly what is necessary to reach the higher initiations as well. The Third Initiation requires a special *mental polarization* or fixed focus, a determined effort to keep one's focus on the mental (vs. the emotional) plane. Such a determined effort will lead you to not only better intuitions and decisions but to higher spiritual contacts as well.

Are you willing to put forth the effort and commitment to find your Path and to be of service? If so, you will become a partner in the work of the progressive unfolding of the Plan. You will begin to work directly with Hierarchy to do your part in this great work. Your intuition will lead you to ever greater service and ever greater rewards.

If you truly desire to serve, meditate regularly on your purpose in life, reflecting on your own personal goals and ideals until you discover your place in life's tapestry. Meditating, reflecting, asking for guidance through dreams and intuitions is the surest way to discover your path. If you sincerely desire to know your path, and sincerely intend to follow it, it *will* be reveled to you.

While you are meditating on your personal goals, meditate on your spiritual goals as well. Are your personal goals aligned with your spiritual goals? If they are not, it will be difficult for you to discover and live your life's purpose. For your individual goals and ideals tell a lot about your true intentions. If you want good for the world, you must be willing to do good in your own life.

Your own values and ideals can lead you to your destiny. Everyone needs to clarify their own ideals, their own values, what is important to them, what they believe in. Your values and ideals are the foundation upon which you build your life. A life without ideals is incomplete; it leads nowhere. Without ideals, without belief in a better world, there is no anchor for your life, no foundation. Your goals become empty, and life can become a dead end street.

Most of us can't live that way. We look for motivation in our lives, not just from without, but from within as well. We are just not happy if we cannot feel good about ourselves. Living up to our personal ideals gives us that inner peace we need to reach other goals.

Many people today - people like you and me - are taking a closer look at their values. We are seeking our ideals. We are looking inward and finding out what is really there.

But, as always, the choice to live our ideals, to serve, is individual. People are opening their hearts and minds to embrace new values. We must choose to reach out into the society in which we live and try to make it a better place for all. And in this quest, each of us has a responsibility, not only to ourselves, but to all those around us. One by one as we each give own special gifts, we are lifting our world to a higher place, to a higher spiritual spiral. By working together we can all eventually outwardly become the spiritual beings that we already are in heart and soul.

## SOME PITFALLS OF THE LIFE OF SERVICE

I would be amiss in this discussion of service if I did not speak to you of some of the pitfalls that challenge an initiate on the Path. A life of service, where you give your gift first for the good of the whole and secondly for yourself, does have its complications and even problems.

First, one must remember that the concept of spiritual "glamour" or illusion exists, even on these levels. You must be constantly on the alert for false ideas, false promises and dead end projects. You may think a certain idea has merit only to realize later that it simply served to take you off your Path, creating a detour of sorts. It is best to think carefully about ideas that you consider to be on your Path, to meditate on their merit, before committing to them. Consider also your motivations for a project or work effort. Are you offering your service out of love or are you experiencing a sense of spiritual "snobbishness" about your giving? Don't fall prey to the *illusion* of spiritual growth. Be always focused first on the group good, and not your own personal reward.

Secondly, don't become so focused on a concept or idea that you lose focus of the purpose behind it. Just as the first example shows the possibility of personal spiritual pride, this example illustrates excessive pride in one's idea or concept.

Again, by keeping the focus off yourself, you'll also keep it off the attachment to your own ideas or plans.

Finally, perhaps the biggest "danger" for serving initiates is the danger of physical overexertion. You can become so determined to give your gift, so singly focused on the Path, that you over-extend your physical self. (This is a tendency that I am unfortunately prone to, but I am working on ways to balance this urge.) There is always an excitement and energy that comes from being on one's Path and serving. It keeps us moving and provides us with a source of energy to do the work. But the energy may even exceed the capabilities of the physical body to handle it. Especially as one goes further on the Path, the energies available to him/her grow ever stronger. One must be careful to take care of the physical body as it is called on to do more and different things than it has ever done.

Paying attention to diet is one thing that I find more important as I move forward on the Path. Never having been inclined toward the health food fads, I resisted looking at this element of my life until I found that I could no longer ignore it. While I used to be able to consume ten cups of caffeinated coffee each day and still sleep at night, now I find that after a few cups I get jittery and lose sleep. I also find that heavy foods like meat and fats seem to bog me down and I feel slow and sluggish after eating them. I am slowly "lightening up" my diet by adding more vegetables and salads and cutting down a bit on the meat and heavy foods. It seems that my higher vibrations are more sensitive to these elements and like it or not, I find that if I want to feel right I have to adjust to the changes.

Rest is another important element during the transformative transition. There were days when I found I couldn't get by without a nap. This was very disconcerting as I had almost every minute scheduled with work. Nonetheless, the tiredness was so strong that I gave in to the urge when necessary and found that it did help. This tired stage lasted about six months and then slowly faded, although it does seem possible that some people who are going through the transformation may even go on to acquire the syndrome called chronic fatigue. Of course, there is no scientific or medical proof of the connection, it is just an observation on my part that the "coincidence" of chronic fatigue in transformers is there. With common sense and precautions, however, I feel that the physical symptoms can be kept to a minimum.

# Chapter 6

# This is a Test... It is Only a Test...

It does seem that in order to serve one must pass a "test." This test consists of something different for every individual, but I am convinced that it is always concerned with the one thing that is most important to you in life at that moment. The test is not easy. It is a true measure of your commitment and your willingness to serve. It is a test of your true intention to let "Thy will be done." To pass the test, you will be made to confront an issue or situation where you must put your commitment to the Plan above all else, even your own happiness (as you see it at that moment.) It seems that for most people during the testing period there is a period of feeling "abandoned" by the sources.

It feels like you are doing your part, but nothing is happening; you are giving your gift, moving forward with your idea of your Plan and you are getting no help. In fact, things seem to be going backwards or falling apart. You wonder if you are in fact on the right Path or if you have made a mistake. You begin to doubt yourself and to think that you have been found lacking and the sources have turned their backs on you. At about this time, you decide that whether or not things go as you had planned or hoped, you will continue to move forward. Even if the sources are not helping, *you* will not give up on what you feel is your duty. Following your intuition, regardless of the consequences, you will move forward; you will continue to live your Plan, being committed to doing God's will (as you intuitively perceive it) even if it means giving up your *conscious* perception of what that would be.

## PERSONAL TESTS

As I said, the test is different for each person. One client who came to me had a test of character, of making a difficult personal decision, which was made even more difficult because it was also associated with several past life experiences. She had to learn to discern which parts of her inclinations were based on current reality and which were based on past karma and to make her decision according to her current life only, even though it was painful to let go of the old ties. This decision ultimately freed her soul to move forward and to focus on the future instead of the past.

Another client's test had to do with weight. She had been overweight for many years but could not seem to do anything about it. Finally in hypnosis we released all past life ties to the tendency to be overweight. In one past life she died in a snowstorm and vowed that from then on would always maintain enough fat to shield her body. In another, she had been a pretty woman in England in the 1800's and a priest had chastised for having too much pride. Her current weight was one way that she was still trying to show this priest that she didn't have too much pride. After releasing these "error messages" and doing other work to work to build up her self-esteem, she decided to let God make the decision about whether she would continue to be heavy or not in this lifetime. She realized that she could now choose to be either way - heavy or thin - and that either would be OK. But she decided that she would turn it over to God and ask that "Thy will be done." By letting go of the struggle, she finally achieved what she had not been able to do with willpower.

While the above "tests" may not appear to be dramatic, believe me they were for the people involved. For each person, the test is not so much in the decision to be made, but in how they go about making that decision. In all cases, the person feels that they have come to a dead end - that they cannot find the right thing to do on their own. The testing comes from whether they decide to listen to outside sources - other people or even their own logical mind - or whether they listen to their inner self - the source of their inner guidance - and most of all, if they are willing to follow that guidance even if it goes against what they *think* they want.

Some of us will have more overtly "spiritual" tests. One woman client felt that her ex-husband was a highly negative and powerful soul. She fought for years to overcome what she perceived to be his "control" over her. When she finally realized that it was *she* who must take control - and responsibility - for what happened to her, she began to release the many painful physical and emotional symptoms that she had carried with her for years (and had sought without much success to find relief from through traditional medical channels.) When she decided to *trust* her own inner guidance, she was able to begin releasing the negative energy she had been holding onto. As the negativity released, her physical symptoms eased as well. We also worked with spiritual healing and chakra energy healing. Today, her condition continues to steadily improve. She is back to work and looking forward to the future for the first time in many years.

My own test involved the dissemination of the learnings that I had acquired during my own spiritual growth. I felt compelled to write down my understandings and share them with others in the form of a book. For several years I thought I would sell this book through traditional sources. Two publishers did, in fact, make an offer to publish the book. But somehow at the last minute, both deals fell through. I began to wonder if I was mistaken in my feeling that I should get this book published. Yet, time after time in my meditations when I asked, "Should I give it up?" the answer was "No. Keep going. It is meant to be." Finally, I told my husband that I was through. I would try to place the book no more. I could not handle the continuous uncertainty. If the book was meant to be, it would find its own way to be published. I was giving up.

I remember well the day I made that decision. I was sitting at my makeup table and reflecting on the problem as I got ready for the day. I said in my heart, *really meaning it*, "Thy will be done." I was committed to following my Path, even if it meant that I should give up the book. I asked God to just show me what He wanted me to do. Not long after, I realized that I had long talked about wanting to get into the publishing business someday, as I enjoyed the business itself almost as much as I enjoyed writing. I realized that I had the potential to be a publisher myself. I had the know-how, I had my markets built in from my years of speaking. I could do it myself.

And so I did. *Tools for Transformation Press* was born. I had never felt so right about a venture as I did about this one. I finally felt at peace about the issue. The decision led to other things - other books, a newsletter, who knows what else. I am still following that Path.

The one thing that was clear, though, from all these experiences with myself and with others, was that *we had to get out of the way first*, before the right decisions could be fully revealed. While we (our personality selves) were still trying to "do it our way" and to make it happen the way we expected it to happen, nothing happened. We had free will and we were using it. Only when *we deferred our will to God's* could the right way reveal itself.

It is scary to let go of our free will. It is scary to say that *no matter what* we will do as we are asked by God. But if we remember that God only does what is best for us, we can relax. Even if what we think we want is not best for us, something better will be given in its place. We just need to trust.

## TRUST

*Trust.* That is one of the big test issues. Many people are working on the need to trust. One client that I worked with was a person with much responsibility, a counselor who made decisions for others all day long as part of her job. But in her own life, she was unable to make decisions. She was afraid of making the wrong one. Only when she learned to get in touch with her inner guidance and to trust that it only made good decisions, was she able to make the life decisions that allowed her to move forward on her Path.

We all need to trust more. Trusting is so hard when you

don't feel in control. But it is only when we can begin to be comfortable with letting go of our need to control that we can feel safe. For safety is really allowing God to *do* and allowing ourselves just to *be*. When we allow the Plan to work *through* us we become one with it and nothing but good can come from that.

## DISCERNMENT

Another lesson of our testing is *discernment* - of learning to discern when we are receiving true intuitive messages. Learning to discern for ourselves what is "truth" and what isn't. Today there is so much "information" available to the seeker. A visit to a regional metaphysical bookstore left my head reeling. There were thousands of titles to choose from. Each offered someone's idea of "truth." But after two hours of looking, I came away with only one book that rang true to me, and even then it contained segments that I could not "buy into." I realized then that I had become truly discerning. I was no longer taken in by claims of "channeled" material. I was not swayed by promises of "enlightenment." I would not be so easily convinced of any "truths." I would instead read and consider and in the end make my own decisions about the truth of the offerings, based on whether or not they felt true according to my inner sensors.

I see now that discernment is a common test. It is one that, along with trust and *patience*, most of us face at the time of transformation.

## PATIENCE

*Patience.* I am not a patient person. I am always moving on to the next project. I am always in a hurry to get to the next challenge. The test of patience was very difficult for me. For four years I felt as if I was holding my breath, knowing that I was to do something, but not knowing how to get it done. Painfully, I learned that the Path itself cannot be hurried. We can hurry along it by choosing the spiritual "fast track," but we cannot make our destinies come any sooner than they are ready to come. Perhaps I could have seen my destiny sooner and passed my test earlier and saved myself some anxiety, but the truth is that the books I write today are different from the one that I first wrote. That first book has been updated, revised and expanded to fit my expanded vision. The book you are currently reading had never even been thought of. I am not the same person, and my Path is not the same. I have moved forward and upward and my Path reflects those changes. Perhaps I had to wait to grow into my destiny.

Patience is not easy to gain. I still don't feel that I truly have it. But I am more inclined to "go with the flow," to "lighten up" and trust that everything will happen according to the Plan in its own time. I do not need to push.

Pushing is resistance. It doesn't feel like resistance, but it is. Pushing is trying to make something happen instead of letting it happen. Pushing shows that we are not fully trusting. So instead of getting what we want, we get more time to earn patience and trust. If instead of pushing we can learn to let go and trust we will find that things move faster and we get where we are going with less pain. That, however, is a lesson that few can learn easily. For most of us there is a time of trying and pushing before we finally "give up" and then, by that act of giving up, finally let go.

## SOUL TESTS

This "giving up" is spoken of in the Alice Bailey books as the *test of the "burning ground."* It is the time when the soul burns its bridges and is released from the hold of the personality. This takes place slowly in the First and Second Initiations when the "fires" of personal goals and desires are sublimated and replaced by group goals or the goals of humanity. Then, at the time of the Third Initiation, the bridge is burned completely and the personality no longer reigns. Instead, forever more the individual is ruled by the desires of the soul.

Another kind of "test" then awaits the progressing and transforming individual. This is the *test of the "clear, cold light,"* or intuitive perception. When one's intuition begins to be their guiding light, they often see for the first time the full range of both good and evil present around them. Intuition brings into their minds more understanding than was ever possible as connections with the higher sources are made. With this realization comes understanding of the possible dangers that one faces by "shining forth" so brightly.

I recall the first time that I fully realized how bright and powerful my light was becoming. Rather than be proud or excited about it, I was terrified. I realized at the same time that there were forces that did not particularly want my light to shine forth - the same forces that had strived to keep mankind in the dark through the use of this very terror since the beginning of time. I felt alone and abandoned once again. I called forth my guides to protect me, but I had little confidence that they would be strong enough to fend off these "dark forces," whose very existence I had for so long refused to recognize. I felt like a pawn in a very old and deadly game.

I could do nothing, it seemed, except go back to the original premise - trust. If the "good guys" were allowing me to shine so brightly they surely would provide me with the protection I needed. Again I asked for help - and received it this time. My mind was relieved of its terror by a calming sense of peace and assurance that all would be well. I felt the presence of much larger forces than I'd ever had - good ones - coming to protect and guide me.

I had passed yet another test - the *test of isolated unity*. I had once again stood my ground, ready to face, alone if need be, the very forces of evil that I knew I could never defeat, trusting that as long as I was on my Path I surely would be doing the right thing. Confident in my decision to stand firm, no matter what, my light drew to me the help I needed. My invocation (plea) was answered. The evocation (answer) came in the form of new and higher guides. I had been admitted into the realm of the Hierarchy. My work was now their work, my Path their Path.

Chapter 7

# ET's and Angels:
# Who Were You Before
# You Were You?

Everyone who makes the transformation to a higher spiritual level - who receives an initiation - will be tested. Personality tests are inevitable and unavoidable. We *must* get ourselves together, release our emotional garbage and let go of past hurts and traumas that keep us focused at the emotional level. We must *move our mental focus, or polarization, up* to the higher chakras and live our lives from our hearts and our souls instead of our emotions.

But there is another kind of reconciliation that must come before we can fully transform. This is the reconciliation with our *soul's* past, a reconciliation of who we were and what we were throughout our many lifetimes that brought us to where we are today.

Many people today believe in past lives, and numbers of

them are re-experiencing their past lives, whether it be sponta-
neously in a dream or a psychic flash, or purposefully in a hypnotic regression (or not so purposefully in a "pop-out" regression during a hypnotic trance for another reason.) I think the
current surge in popularity surrounding past lives is more than
curiosity; it is a result of a need to find out who and what we
were in order to integrate this knowledge at a conscious level.

Our souls have always known who we were. From lifetime
to lifetime your soul carries your personality thread, bringing
with it the learnings from a previous lifetime or existence. But
this has always been happening below the level of waking consciousness, at the soul level. Now, for the first time ever, we are
being challenged to gain full awareness of our soul's legacy. We
are being guided to realize our pasts and to accept them, to
integrate our past selves into our current selves at a conscious
level.

Why is it so important to *consciously* recognize our soul's
heritage? Because unless we accept ourselves - and our souls -
completely, we cannot transform. Just as we must cleanse our
personality selves of old emotional "garbage," so must we cleanse
our souls, accepting and loving all that we were on our long
journey to here.

It may be difficult to accept some parts of who we were.
But we have all been or will be everything that there is to be.
We will all experience the full range of human experience. This
means that we will all have some tragic lives and some happy
lives, some lives where we are kind and good people, some
lives where we are not so good. Whether thief, liar, king or
peasant all these experiences lead us to know life better and
therefore helped our souls to grow. Some of us may have even
experienced other kinds of existences, not on the earth plane.

These experiences, too, are a part of our soul's legacy and must be accepted as a part of who we are.

Past life remembrances can help us to integrate these past soul parts with the whole. Just as some of us have more emotional healing to do, some of us, too, have more soul healing to do. Some past life remembrances come to help us heal old emotional wounds from previous lives that kept us from fully learning the lessons of that lifetime. Other times, as in my own case, they come to reconcile a past that has been kept in the closet for aeons of time unrecognized - and therefore unavailable - as a resource to the consciously emerging soul.

Without the barriers between the personality and the soul at the Third Initiation, it becomes necessary for the individual to make peace with his or her soul's past, to recognize and integrate all the soul fragments that remain outside the whole. Most of these fragments are integrated naturally within the soul's evolution. If the soul faces no conflict as the personality awareness grows, the soul fragments can simply integrate the learnings from each lifetime into the new personality as personality traits, character traits or innate talents or tendencies. When, however, there is a conflict or trauma that is too severe to integrate, or when the soul itself decides that certain knowledge or experience should be held back until further evolvement would make it better able to be successfully integrated, then the soul will suppress that information. Just as in our subconscious minds we can "hide" things from ourselves, so can our soul - for its own growth - "hide" knowledge from itself until it is ready to fully integrate it in the best possible way.

## YOU MAY BE MORE THAN YOU THINK

I've always thought of myself as an "average" person, more or less. Oh, I knew there was something a little different about me, but I figured that my difficult childhood contributed to my intensity of nature and seriousness. As a child I felt like a very old person. I seemed to be able to understand things beyond my years. I could understand other people's problems, even though they might be quite different from my own. Older friends would seek my advice on relationships or life choices. Although I recall little of my childhood, having suppressed much of it, I do recall an overall feeling of being very old inside. I sometimes felt like I was just waiting for time to pass, so my body would grow and I could begin to "do my job."

I recall at age thirteen feeling very lonely and helpless, wondering if I could hang on for another five years. During one of my many solitary walks I heard a voice *outside myself* say, "You have a job to do and it has to do with how the universe works." Then inside my head other messages began to come forth. I was told that the first thing I needed to do was, in essence, to get myself "together" emotionally.

Since then, I've been led to new tasks and "jobs," always via an intuitive message that is so strong that I know it must be heeded. That first message set me on my Path. I've found many surprises along the way. Once in a workshop in Dayton, Ohio, I met another speaker with whom I immediately identified. We both felt a rapport as if our energies had connected. During my speech, I felt a pouring of universal energy come into my body and flow out into the audience. I realize now that this other person's energy had been a catalyst to finally open my solar plexus chakra all the way. Not only that, this person was on my Path for another reason. Through her I learned about hypnotherapy and knew immediately that this was something that I should do. Three days later I was enrolled in my first hypnotherapy class which led to much of my current knowledge and to my decision to pursue a degree in social work so that I might share my work with a broader audience.

But aside from the personal path this turn of events led me to an even more profound change, and a level of growth that I would have never dreamed possible. During one of my advanced hypnotherapy courses, we were learning the technique of doing past life regressions. I had never considered getting a past life regression myself, even though I had been teaching spiritual classes for about eight years. My reasoning was that I didn't have any unexplained problems that would lead me to believe that a traumatic past life needed to be cleared up. And besides, I hadn't found anyone who I felt I could trust to do it (even though I knew of a psychologist who did past life regressions). Nonetheless, at this point, want it or not, I was getting a past life regression, as we students always "practiced" on one another.

Six weeks before the day of the regression I began to experience intense anxiety whenever I thought about the upcoming event. I was inexplicably tense, literally "shaking in my boots." Not only that, I began to have a feeling of dread and a reoccurrence of childhood nightmares where lights filled the sky. I knew that these were UFO's and that they had come to get me (among other people also huddled behind the large rocks in the field.) My biggest fear was that I would be leaving my family behind, abandoning them and being myself alone.

Shortly before the weekend of the past life regression, we did another hypnotherapy session where the technique was to deal with the biggest fear in your life. At the time I wasn't thinking about the UFO dream but was shocked and terrified to go into a hypnotic vision of seeing a spaceship and a little man coming out and walking toward me. I was so fearful that my partner had to incorporate several "safety" techniques to allow me to feel comfortable enough to talk to him (we put him behind plexiglass and kept him at a distance). He told me that I had a job to do (a familiar phrase) and that even though I was afraid, that I should not worry because I had previously *agreed* to do this job, in full knowledge of what it entailed. I had made a commitment and a sacrifice which I was just now fully realizing. Then he left.

Immediately, within my body there was a deep relaxation, a sigh of relief. If I had made a promise, fine; I would keep it. I knew instinctively that this would have some later connection to the past life regression, but now I was resigned to it. My extreme sense of commitment to keeping promises was a life-long value. I also knew that this commitment would lead me to a positive place, no matter how scary it might be to get there.

Too soon, the weekend of the regression came and with it the return of my fears. Yes, I would go through with it, but not happily. That Friday evening as I arrived in Dayton I was a nervous wreck. The next morning we were going to do the technique. That night as I was lying in my bed in my hotel room, studying, I was suddenly overcome by the feeling of a "presence" trying to reach me. I knew that in a moment's time I could be channeling this presence and finding out what it wanted, but I felt very anxious about making the contact. Some intuition told me that it had to do with the regression and I wanted to wait and deal with that when I had my fellow students as "protection." But the presence was so intense and so distracting that I finally thought, "Ok, let me just let in a little bit of it so that I can drain off some of this excess energy and then I can get back to work." No sooner had the thought ended when I was overcome by a vision of being in a forest. Only I wasn't just seeing the vision, I was *in* it.

I was looking up into the sky. Just ahead at treetop level was a large white light. It was a UFO but it was *going,* not coming. I was overwhelmed with grief. I was sobbing, crying baskets of tears, reaching out in pitiful desperation. "They're leaving me! They're leaving me behind! My people! My people! They're leaving me behind!" I cried over and over, sobbing into my pillow so as not to wake my neighbors.

About this time, as some fragment of my conscious mind was grasping the meaning of these words, I began to envision and to *feel* the physical presence of an ET. He was similar to the "Gumby" types depicted in some books - long, thin body, tendril like fingers, and an egg shaped head. He had wonderful, loving, large dark eyes. He was just in front of me and to my left. He was telling me "I'm sorry. I'm so sorry. I never wanted to leave you. We tried to wait for you but we couldn't any longer." (Evidentially if an ET lingered too long in earth's dense vibrations, their own vibrations would decrease as well and they could become "held" by earth's magnetic field.) "You knew this was a possibility," he continued, "when you accepted the task." (To "seed" the earth - I got the impression that this was millions of years ago at the dawn of life on earth). "You agreed to take the risk," he reminded me. "But I always loved you. I didn't leave you on purpose. I missed you so much."

Then he began to touch my face, my arms, my hands and to caress me as a loved one would. He told me that he was my father and that it was he who had visited me in the previous hypnotic session. He said that the time had come for me to realize who and what I was and to reclaim my heritage.

Forget it! That's what I thought. No way did I want to be an ET. I'd worked very hard in my life to maintain an image of "normalcy" as I went about my metaphysical work. My traditional image lent credibility to my work as did my research and writing. I didn't want it "spoil" my image by claiming such a way out idea.

But the trance had been so immediate, so strong and so undeniable that I had no choice but to entertain the possibility that it might be true. The next day I revisited the scene and went through a somewhat less traumatic version. (Luckily, too, for the rest of the group!) "Frederick" (not his real name he said, but what I could call him) said that if I would allow it that he could become a part of my aura and be with me from that moment on to guide me and to help me. I agreed (sort of) and then he began to hang around in my aura, at about the level of my right shoulder. It felt kind of comforting to have him there and I came to enjoy it. About a year later, I came to *fully* accept him and he now resides in me and is truly a part of me. (I feel him in my heart.)

This final merging took place in a semi-dream state as I was falling off to sleep one night. I had done a healing technique on a client that day and had been led to "circulate" her chakra energies. I mention this because she, too, began to experience the process that I am about to describe, but for her, we have yet to find the reason (unless it was just that having been so closely connected via our chakras earlier, she just "picked up" on my energies). At any rate, pretty much "out of the blue" I began to experience a movement of energy within my chakras, starting at the base of my spine. I guess you might call it a "kundilini rising" effect. I felt a vibration in each chakra in turn, starting with the first and going through the seventh, with a continuing rising up of the energies from each chakra below as the process continued. I had done chakra exercises and had felt the move of kundilini energy before, but this was happening without my even having to focus my attention on the areas. The effect was so strong this time that it woke me up. As the energy flowed upward it would "stop" for a few moments at each chakra. I felt through this process a sense of integration, of finally having full energy flow available between all chakras. I knew instinctively that this experience would lead to positive results, but I had no clue as to what they might be.

As the final crown chakra was integrated, I felt "Frederick" move from my aura into my body, first overlaying me and then settling down into my heart. I felt totally at peace with this move and accepted him wholly. At that moment I realized that I had accepted and integrated a previously separated part of my soul. Now my soul was whole.

## ARE YOU AN ET, AN ANGEL, OR BOTH?

As I have come to accept my "heritage," (I realized that not only had I dealt with my biggest fear, but that fear was what I had really wanted all along. Some sort of cosmic joke?) I have come to realize that I really had no reason to fear. This alone was worth the price of the course! It also pointed out a universal truth - there is nothing to fear but fear itself. What energy I had wasted on unwarranted fear!

Since learning of my space relations I have pieced together some fragments of memories form the past that now make sense. A UFO siting with my sister, a strange obsession with UFO books as a teen, anxiety during UFO movies along with a strange compulsion to watch them, mysterious nosebleeds, and, of course, the nightmares.

If you saw *Close Encounters of the Third Kind* and felt an affinity with it, you, too may be in for a surprise someday. It appears that UFO's may have come to Earth many times to help us earthlings (and I use that term loosely for some of us) to fulfill our destinies. We cannot forget the fact that what happens here on Earth affects other planets and other beings in the universe as well. It is important to the vast universal family that each and every member transform and grow spiritually. Each turn of the spiral allows others both above and below us to transform as well.

Knowing this, is it not likely that those of us who perhaps have some ancient ties with these universe brothers would be the ones whose job it is to finish what was started so long ago and to assure that humanity evolves to the next level? As a possible ET, you may have certain signs that you will be awakening to that will help you accept your heritage - and your job.

## ET'S PHONE HOME

Do you have a heritage as an ET? Here are the ten most common indicators of an ET experience, taken from the book, *Encounters* by psychologist and hypnotherapist Edith Fiore, Ph.D. If you have had an ET encounter and recognize any of these symptoms, chances are that you have an ET heritage as well:

- Missing time.

- Nightmares and/or dreams about UFOs or aliens.

- Sleep disorders.

- Waking up with unusual body sensations.

- Unexplained marks on the body.

- Feeling watched, monitored, or communicated with.

- Repeated UFO sightings.

- Vague recollection of encounter(s).

- Unexplained healing.

- Fear of or anxiety about UFOs or ET's.

Even though I now believe that my ET heritage is possibly very real, it does not significantly color my life. If anything, it has reduced my UFO curiosity. I still feel that my job is to be a "voice of reason" in the metaphysical field. I accept and *value* my ET heritage, for with its acceptance have come many new spiritual "gifts," including my blossoming healing powers.

I think that perhaps we all have, at some distant time, had extra-planetary lives. The objective appears to be to broaden our experiences, to make us better prepared for our future tasks and to facilitate the final emergence of our souls.

## OH, YOU'RE SUCH AN ANGEL

Now that you may be more accepting of the thought of ET's, what about those angels? We all have seen the influx of angel books and angel pins, angel calenders and angel ornaments. What's it all about? As I mentioned earlier, I think that this may be a result of an awakening to yet another heritage - our angelic soul fragments.

Some of us may even have been angels, it seems. Some define angels as those who have never been incarnated into a human life (that was always my definition). But others define "angels" more broadly. Solara, in *The Star Borne,* describes all who are acting as "anchors for the light" of the new energy as angels. She states that we who are working to bring about the planetary transformation (initiation) are actually transforming ourselves - into angels! We are experiencing a restructuring of our DNA (attributed to the effects of the higher frequencies of the new energy within our bodies).

Until a while ago, such an idea would have seemed far fetched to me. But when I read this I recalled that several years prior a member of my meditation group who also channeled had predicted a "restructuring of our DNA" as a part of the changes that we were about to encounter. Truthfully, at the time I took this message with a rather large grain of salt. But when things appear in three's I begin to listen. And for the third time, I subsequently read in *Bringers of the Dawn,* by Barbara Marciniak, the channeled message that there would, indeed, be an "evolution of our DNA." This evolution would bring "memories flooding back into our consciousnesses." Certain DNA codes would be triggered to "bring into the forefront full realization of our soul's heritage." I found it no coincidence that I picked up Barbara's book shortly after my ET regression. The signs are there for me, but you must decide for yourself (remember discernment?). Are you an angel or an angel in the making? If you are reading such books as *The Star Borne* and this very book in your hands, you may be being guided to realize your heritage, to wake up to who you really are.

Here are the "angel signs" mentioned in *The Star Borne* by Solara:

- Tiredness.

- Strange cravings or change in eating habits (often toward lighter, more healthy foods).

- Ringing in the ears (someone trying to get through?).

- A feeling of higher vibratory rate (nervousness or "jazzed" feeling).

- Possible shortness of breath or erratic heartbeat.

(Note the similarities between this list and the "transformation symptoms" list in the first pages of this book.)

Whether or not you are an angel, an ET or both, many of you are apparently here for a purpose. You are *transformers*, pioneers of a new way of being that will bring about Planetary Initiation.

If you feel a kinship with the messages within this book, welcome to the spiritual fast lane! Your challenge now, as was mine, is to wake up to the call. To accept it and to *consciously* go about fulfilling your part in the unfoldment of the new spiritual era. Embracing your soul's mission with full understanding and commitment, you join the others who herald the New Age.

# Chapter 8

# Planetary Initiation

By listening to our intuition, each of us can become aware of our individual Paths. We can understand our personal Purpose in life and strive to fulfill it. But we are not individual consciousnesses, isolated and alone. Each of us is a part of a bigger life, a larger Purpose. There is a greater Plan that enfolds each of our individual plans and even as we barely begin to glimpse our own personal destinies, we are at the same time furthering the Planetary Plan and Purpose.

What is the plan for our planet? What is our united destiny? According to the ancient esoteric texts, the Plan and the Purpose of the planet are embodied in the *beings* of the highest spiritual entities that deal with our planet - one being Sanat Kumara, the "Lord of the World," and the others being the members of the Council of Shamballa (our highest spiritual plane). Only these highest sources of spiritual energy are knowledgeable of the true destiny of our world, of the purpose of evolution and of the Plan for allowing these to come about.

Little has been revealed about the Plan and the Purpose because of fear that the "dark forces" might use this information for their evil purposes. Now that mankind is evolving and we are raising our spiritual natures to a higher plane, the Plan is slowly being revealed. The Purpose behind the Plan, however, may never be made available to humans. We must wait until we have reached higher spiritual levels than Earth life can offer. The process of spiritual unfoldment has always been to reveal just enough of the Path to allow students to progress.

## THE PLANETARY PLAN

This I have gleaned from the *Alice Bailey Books* about the Plan of our planet:

- The planet is a living being. It is the *body* of Sanat Kumara.

- The planet itself is evolving.

- As each individual evolves, humanity as a whole evolves.

- The evolution of the human kingdom makes possible the evolution of the animal, plant and mineral kingdoms below it, as well as the evolution of the kingdoms above it (Hierarchy and Shamballa).

- The evolution and spiritual growth of all kingdoms comes about as a result of the use of the *Will energy*.

Let's look at each of these ideas in turn:

### The Planet Is a Living Being

For most of us the thought of the planet as being alive is seen as the concept of "Mother Earth," or the Gaia principle. We can accept a "synergy" effect in evolution. We can accept that all things (even "dead things" such as rocks) have a form of consciousness. Many of us talk to our plants. We have opened our minds to a wider view of life than ever before. But for most of us - and that included me - the thought of the earth as an actual *being* seems rather amazing. Yet, after having even limited direct contact with the higher sources I have come to accept the above statement. The planet is a living being. "It" has a personality. It is the actual "body" of Sanat Kumara, a living spiritual being. (Sanat Kumara does not have human life, of course, but a form of spiritual life that can transform itself into matter at will and that out of *service* embodied as our planet to serve as our training ground "until the last weary traveler finds his way home.")

One might wonder at the logic of such statements but obviously, at some level (not far above the level of human mental capacity) logic breaks down. There are ways of being and orders of creativity that our limited minds cannot begin to fathom. All that we can do is to have faith in the integrity of the Masters whose jobs it is to reveal the Truth.

### The Planet Itself Is Evolving

Few of us would doubt that evolution takes place *on* the planet. But what you might not have thought about is that evolution takes place *in* the planet. As the planet's "tenants" evolve so does their "host." As a living being, Sanat Kumara, the Lord of the World, is on a quest to further his own spiritual evolution, just as you and I are. Even though he may be far ahead of us in his spiritual journey, he is still not at his "final" destination either. There is little information about the life and destiny of Sanat Kumara, but I do know that we, humanity, are considered to be the equivalent of his throat chakra, and that as we evolve Sanat Kumara's throat chakra is opened.

### As Each Individual Evolves,
### Humanity as a Whole Evolves

We are connected; there is no getting around it. Previously there may have appeared to be separateness because the First and Second Initiations were taken individually up to this point. But today these initiations are being administered to groups - to large numbers of humanity at the same time. Just as there must be a "crisis point" for leaps in evolution to take place, there must be a crisis point in the lives of enough individual humans to allow for group initiation to take place. Feeling a spiritual need, we cry out for help. Many voices sounding together have created a united plea for help, a *group invocation*, that was registered and is now being responded to by the Hierarchy. This has resulted in the first ever decision to allow for group initiation.

### The Evolution of Humanity Makes Possible
### The Evolution of The Kingdoms Above and Below It

We learn in the Bible that man has "dominion" over the other kingdoms on earth - the mineral, plant and animal kingdoms. So far we seem to have taken that phrase to mean that we can *dominate* the other kingdoms, but that is not what was really intended. Dominion really means responsibility for, rather than control over, these lower kingdoms. Just as the Hierarchy oversees our evolution and lovingly nurtures it, we are meant to lovingly nurture the evolution of the *consciousnesses* below ours. I think that we had better wake up and begin to see the lesser kingdoms as they really are - life evolving - and not as our own personal creative clay to mold as we see fit.

Even as we must claim responsibility for the lesser kingdoms we must also recognize our responsibility to the kingdoms above us. As we evolve we are expected to do our share to help assure the evolution of others. Initiates (those who have reached the Third Initiation level) can and must begin to work with Hierarchy to assure that Planetary Initiation is successful. Only then will certain members of Hierarchy be free to "move up" to their next level and be replaced by incoming souls who have finally been freed from the wheel of karma. So the process goes. Each move forward by one soul helps "bump" a soul above it up a notch as well.

### The Evolution and Spiritual Growth of All Kingdoms Comes About as a Result of the Use of the Will Energy

Evolution is purposeful. Whether you see the act of evolution arising from a nurturing "mother earth" or from the deliberate and loving actions of a benevolent spirit being, life and evolution are no accident. But in order to have purpose, you must have will, an intention to do something. Where does the Will energy come from and what is it really?

There was an interesting theory set out by scientist Arthur

Young in his book, The *Reflexive Universe*. His theory states that consciousness is itself a product of the Will energy, or life force, and that this consciousness/Will manifests itself as *light*. This corresponds directly to a statement in *The Rays and the Initiations* that evolution is the "raising up, or the transition from the darkness of matter to the light of spirit," and that this is done through "the right use of the Will."

Young envisioned that his theory of consciousness could explain not only the personal consciousnesses of people, but the *consciousness of evolution* as well. Young saw evolution as a process that provided a framework from within which *transformation* could logically take place. He saw transformation as the purpose of life. He saw the life force as energy or *action*, not matter, and compared it to decision or *intent*. Light itself was seen as a living thing with consciousness and purpose. Light may be the only element of the Divine Purpose that most of us encounter and yet we can easily miss its significance.

## THE IMPORTANCE OF LIGHT

Think for a moment about the function and purpose of light in our lives. Light is the giver of life. Light makes it possible for life to exist on earth. Without light there would be no heat, no elements, chemical reactions, no plants, no photosynthesis, no evolution, no life. Light, it seems, is fundamental. Said a little differently, light could be *first cause*, the origin of all things. In many creation myths light stands out as the initial ingredient necessary to start the process of life. Light also is a spiritual element, representing the idea of illumination or decision. In the Mayan and Zuni Indian creation myths it is the creator's decision or thought that first creates the light. In the Bible it says, "And God said, 'Let there be light' and there was light." There is also reference to God himself as the "Light of the world."

Light embodies not only illumination and decision, but action as well. Life undulates and vibrates with motion. It is this "act of action" that manifests itself as light. Is light, then, the life force? There is some indication that it is. Light takes many forms. It is light as *consciousness* that oversees the unfolding of evolution. (You should note here that although in the *Alice Bailey Books* there is a distinction made between the sutratma, or life force thread, and the consciousness thread itself, Young's theory combines the two.)

Arthur Young described life as unfolding through seven stages or "kingdoms" and his theory showed that in order for each kingdom to evolve - from light to nuclear particles, to atoms, to molecules, to the plant and animal kingdoms up to the "kingdom" of man - a deliberate *decision* had to be made. This decision involved each kingdom giving up some of its creative and expanding potential in order to allow for the upward evolution of the next kingdom after it. For instance, the kingdom of light gave up its unlimited potential for freedom and allowed itself to become "bound" into nuclear energy and atoms. Light and nuclear energy were then restricted further when they merged into atoms and gave up more of their freedom in order to evolve into matter, then the various chemical elements and all the material forms that we know today.

According to Young, these "decisions" were, like human initiations, involuntary and "pre-programmed." But at the point of the molecular level *the decision to evolve became a voluntary one*. Mere combinations, it seems, no matter how complex, did not make up life. It took organization of molecules into systems (like organs) that carried out a specific purpose to create the process of life. This new factor of *organization*, Young postulated, came about as a result of *free will* held within the consciousness of life itself. He called this *conscious* move of evolution from determinism to free will, from non-life to life, *the turn*.

## MANKIND'S TURNING POINT

Not only did the early stages of the evolution of light into life depend upon a free will decision, so even now do the continuing stages of evolution of mankind depend on a free will decision - the decision to *transform*. Each of us at the Third Initiation will face our own *turning point*. We will be faced with the decision to continue our spiritual unfoldment and make a commitment to all that comes with it.

Like the kingdoms below us, it will be up to us to decide whether we will move our focus from our personal selves to the group, from personal advancement and "success seeking" to a mindset of service and giving. (The strange thing is, though, that once you make this decision and are guided to your Path and begin to live your destiny, you will often find that "success" you longed for, even if it comes in a slightly different package.) Once you move from an ego consciousness to a soul consciousness you will find that your priorities often change, but that you are happier with them. You are more at peace, yet more productive and creative. It sometimes takes a risk to live your destiny, but you will never regret the decision.

Now is the time. As your ego fully develops, it must decide where it ends. It must decide when its need must give way and allow the soul to take over. Just as in the kingdoms below us, we humans must forgo unlimited individual expansion to allow for the survival of the group, and to ensure future evolution. This "surrender" may not come easily, but at some point, if not in this lifetime then in another, this will happen for each of us.

This is *the turn*. The choice is individual, personal, but it affects the whole. In the mind of each individual human being on earth today lies all hope for humanity.

## WHAT COMES NEXT?

As we evolve and develop our soul consciousness, we are "moving up" on the spiritual spiral. Even as we move up, so do members of the Hierarchy and Shamballa, and members of the lower kingdoms. Is it not believable that this whole process is a part of an intricate and well organized Plan, with a fuller Purpose behind it? Even if we don't fully understand the Plan and the Purpose, through *faith* we dedicate ourselves to it. If we decide to set aside our personal wills and to defer to the Divine Will, then we will become working partners with Hierarchy; we will be "admitted" to its outer realms, ever closer and ready to move fully into participation at our Fourth Initiation. This we can do if we can truly and with conscious knowledge of its full significance say, "*Not my will but Thy Will be done.*"

The Will energy, of which our personal wills are but a faint reflection, holds the Purpose and guides the Plan. Evolution comes about through right use of the Will. The Will energy is without a doubt the most important source of energy available to mankind. It is closely related to the life force energy and *through the activation of the first and seventh chakras, the Will energy is circulated.* As we tread our personal paths and become more knowledgeable, and gain deeper recognitions of the Plan, we will begin to learn how to better wield the energies and forces available to us through these potent universe sources - the life force thread and the consciousness thread which carries the Will energy. Careful study of the chakra systems and their potential for creative and healing powers will be the object of serious metaphysical students.

With a broader realization of what thoughts, intentions and the Will really are - cosmic *energy* capable of great creative endeavors - the student will begin to awaken to his full potential as a *creator and a custodian of the future*. When the *light* of illumination and intuitive understanding fully take hold within the student's mind, he will begin to fulfill his destiny. This destiny will not only affect his own future but the future of the rest of the universe as well.

## THE TRANSFORMATION PROCESS

Once you have awakened to the call, you can begin the journey of personal and planetary transformation, and take part in the Planetary Initiation. Let us review the phases of the transformation process so that you can fully acknowledge where you are now and where you are headed, so that you can make a full and knowledgeable choice about whether to move forward at this time.

- First, there is the *call* or urge to grow. You find yourself a seeker, a student perhaps of the metaphysical or some other esoteric philosophy. (First Initiation.)

- Then comes a point when you realize that you can't go on any further without making a change. You've come to a "dead end." You've "stagnated." Or perhaps you've come to realize that there are blocks that you must clear away before you can move forward on your personal Path.

- You (reluctantly perhaps) decide to "clean house" emotionally and deal with old issues that are holding you back. (Second Initiation as lower chakras are prepared for the "move up" when your focus of attention will "rise" to the higher chakras and you will respond to life from the heart and head instead of from your emotional nature.)

- You begin to move forward spiritually and realize that there is "help" available from guides, angels or other spiritual sources. You realize that these sources are monitoring your progress and are guiding you and urging you ever forward.

- You learn to make contact with these sources and learn that you must make a *conscious* commitment to your Path in order to continue further.

- You either do this and say with full understanding and intention, "Thy Will, not mine, be done." (Third Initiation and your personal "turning point," at which time you receive the "Initiation Ceremony" and begin building your personal antahkarana which will be part of the planetary antahkarana). Or you delay this committment and remain a dedicated student but without further responsibilities, rewards or higher spiritual contacts.

- You experience the transformation symptoms and tests and "prove" both your willingness and your ability to serve. (Most transformation symptoms eventually disappear, many within six months.)

- You recognize the "presence" of the new energy within your body as it aligns your vibrations with its own, increasing your vibrations and making your body available as a "step down" unit to ease the entry of the new energy into the bodies of others. (This happens as your auras meet and whenever you come into contact with other people, so you begin to be led to "go out into the world" more, and you find that your Path often leads you there.)

- You continue to dedicate your life to *service* and furthering both the Plan and the Purpose. Your life is ever more directed by intuition and you have ever more contact with the higher spiritual sources, Masters and members of Hierarchy, and even Shamballa. They will provide you with everything you need to continue your work.

If you decide to make *the turn*, to continue your spiritual growth, to take part in the transformation process and to become counted within the outer ranks of Hierarchy, you will not be sorry that you did. Even though the tests are hard and the road is long, it is worth the trip. You will be rewarded for your efforts.

You will receive spiritual "gifts" such as healing techniques, intuitive understandings and spiritual "lessons." You will receive anything and everything that you need to follow your Path and do your chosen work or service. (I often get asked by students about how they might learn to be healers. The best advice I can give them is to go through the transformation process!) Without even having to ask, your spiritual gifts will be given to you.

These gifts will "arrive" intuitively, so you must ever be conscious of you own intuitive voices. You must stay true to your intentions that "Thy Will be done." You must continue to nurture the attitude of service and allow your soul to remain in control at all times (in so far as that is humanly possible).

If you can pass the tests (and no test is given that you cannot pass if the desire and intention is there) then you will make it through the "burning grounds" and will find a sense of peace and oneness that makes it all worthwhile. You will have met your dragons and tamed them. You will have claimed your soul's heritage. You will now be ready to claim your future - as a *conscious creator*. You will learn to wield your emerging power lovingly and wisely for the greater good of mankind - and for the vast universal family of which you are a part.

I encourage you to take part in this exciting unfoldment. Dare to become. Dare to transform. Help bring about the sacred spiritual act of *Planetary Initiation*.

# Index

# Workshops by Rita Milios

- *Tools for Transformation* - Learn first-hand how to use the "rules" and "tools" of the subconscious realm to transform your life for good.

- *Planetary Initiation* - Based on the book by the same name, this workshop covers the major points, with personal anecdotes and advice.

- *Healing through the Body's Energy Systems* - Healing techniques from visualization and guided imagery to aura and chakra healing.

- *Connecting With Your Creative Center* - Using meditation, dreams and other subconscious tools to get inspiration, problem-solving and creativity at will.

- *Positive Self-Imaging* - How to change your thinking and change your life by re-programming negative attitudes and acquiring a mind-set of personal power.

A member of the National Speakers Association, **Rita Milios** has delivered dynamic, hands-on workshops for eight years to audiences nationwide, including professional counselors, teachers, students and lay people from all walks of life. She is listed in *Who's Who in American Women*, *The International Who's Who of Professional and Business Women*, *Something About the Author* and other professional listings. Her therapeutic guided imageries have been published in *Guided Imagery, Volume 4*. She is a Certified Hypnotherapist and Hypno-anaesthesia Technician.

**Rita Milios** is available for these and other workshops.

Call or write Rita c/o *Tools for Transformation Press*
7150 Cloister Rd. W. • Toledo, OH 43617
Ph. (419) 841-4657.

# Books and Tapes
# by Rita Milios

## BOOKS @ $9.95

*Planetary Initiation*     Initiation is the age old process of progressing forward on a spiritual spiral. For the first time in history, Initiation is available to all people, making possible exciting and positive growth and also creating "tests" that we must overcome. Find out which Initiation you are working on and how you can best assure your own - and the planet's - growth.

*Tools for Transformation*     Learn step-by-step how to use the powerful mind tools of affirmations, visualizations, meditations, dreams and positive thinking. Learn to make better use of your "programming" ability. Learn the three types of meditation and why you should be using them all. Become more successful, healthier and happier by letting go of old mental "programs" that hold you back. Take charge of the potential within your own mind.

*Intuition Log Book*     Log in and assess your hunches, synchronicities and intuitions. Discover your unique intuition cues. Train your intuition as you log!

*Dream Journal*     Keep track of your dreams, including dream themes, characters and messages. Analyze dreams over time for greater insight.

## TAPES @ $9.95

Daily Meditation / Positive Affirmations

Mind/Body Healing / Forgiveness Visualization

Guides, Angels and Other Helpers / Meet Your Guides Visualization

Becoming Your Full Potential Self / Full Potential Self Visualization

Chakras and Energy Fields / Chakra Balancing Visualization

Weight Loss Meditation / Exercises, Visualizations

# Book and Tape Order Form

## Books @ $9.95

1. Planetary Initiation          3. Dream Journal

2. Tools for Transformation      4. Intuition Log

## Tapes @ $9.95

A. Daily Meditation / Positive Affirmations

B. Mind/Body Healing / Forgiveness Visualization

C. Guides, Angels, Helpers / Guide Visualization

D. Full Potential Self / FPS Visualization

E. Chakras / Chakra Visualization

F. Weight Loss Meditation / Exercises, Visualizations

| Book/Tape | Quantity | Price | Total |
|-----------|----------|-------|-------|
| _____ | _____ | _____ | _____ |
| _____ | _____ | _____ | _____ |
| _____ | _____ | _____ | _____ |
| _____ | _____ | _____ | _____ |

Postage: Add $1.50 for first book or tape; 75 cents for each additional book or tape. Send check or money order to: Tools for Transformation Press, 7150 Cloister Rd. W. • Toledo, OH 43617

Postage: _____
**Grand Total:** _____

## Tools for Transformation Press
7150 Cloister Rd. W. • Toledo, OH 43617 (419) 841-4657

*Rita Milios*, hypnotherapist, author, workshop leader and spiritual teacher has experienced her own "transformation" and has helped others to experience theirs. Author of *Tools for Transformation* and sixteen other books for adults and children, Rita combines a knowledge of religion, philosophy, psychology, science and metaphysics to bring to her readers a clearer understanding of personal transformation, choice and spirituality. She is currently researching the connection between self-actualization and spirituality and is pursuing a Masters Degree in Social Work.

---

# Let Us Hear From You

We'd like to hear your comments and suggestions. If this book has been useful to you, please let us know:

- In what ways did you implement the teachings of this book into your life?

- Do you have suggestions or ideas for future books, tapes or workbooks?

- Do you have a group or association which would be interested in a workshop by Rita Milios? Can you suggest Healing Centers in your area that Rita Milios might want to contact?

Your comments, suggestions and help are appreciated. If you would like to receive a **free kit,** *Starting Your Own Light Group,* please send a 9x12 SASE with 75 cents postage with your comments or ideas.

Write Rita Milios c/o *Tools for Transformation Press*
7150 Cloister Rd. W. • Toledo, OH 43617